MAP of DESIRE

6.13.15

For Allan,

May this book help you
enliven your "gun-lap of your
life. You're well on your
way!

F.v. Smg

MAP of DESIRE

BLUEPRINT FOR SELF-FULFILLMENT

•

FU-DING CHENG

MAP OF DESIRE
Blueprint for Self-Fulfillment

Published by
Waterfront Digital Press
Cardiff, California   92007

First Edition, First Printing

Library of Congress Cataloging-In-Publication Data is available upon request.

ISBN (paperback) 978-1-939116-91-8
ISBN (eBook) 978-1-629213-67-5

Printed in the USA

"The greatest adventure
anyone can embark upon
is to look within."

CONTENTS

FOREWORD BY DON MIGUEL RUIZ   11

PREFACE   13

ACKNOWLEDGMENTS   17

INTRODUCTION   19

PART ONE • THE JOURNEY BEGINS   25

Chapter 1: Being   27
This first chapter portrays the Source of the universe and everything in it including all humans. Though free of all visible forms, Being teems with consciousness, energy, and love.

Chapter 2: Etheric Body   37
From vast, abstract Being, the first glimmerings of an individual comes through the etheric body, the manifestation of a human soul.

Chapter 3: The Human Form   43
This chapter shows the formation of the *Emotional, Mental* and *Physical Bodies* of a human, as well as the development of instruments of consciousness including the *Heart* and *Mind*, *Intuition* and *Reason*.

PART TWO • LOST AND CONFUSED   **51**

Chapter 4: Challenges of Life   53

In a close-up, this map focuses on the strategic area of the *Heart* and *Mind.* It shows an individual's first reaction to the unrelenting challenges of life beginning with instinctual desires.

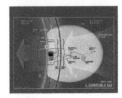

Chapter 5: Formation of Ego   61

This blueprint portrays how we meet the ever-growing challenges of life through the formation of the ego. Key components include the *Judge, Victim, Self* and *Public Image.*

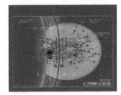

Chapter 6: Tyranny of Desire   77

This map depicts the present condition of the typical human (and contemporary society). Ego-driven and materialistic, we're inundated with a confusing array of overlapping and contradictory desires.

PART THREE • FINDING OUR WAY OUT   **87**

Chapter 7: Attunement to Being   89

This chapter reveals the first of three clear pathways towards personal freedom. Cutting through the demands of the ego, we reconnect to our source in Being.

Chapter 8: Detachment from Outcomes   101

Here we see how detachment helps us to gain equanimity over the ups and downs of life. We become free of the world of appearances.

Chapter 9: Healing the Wounds   111

In this map, we address the last of the three pathways that can lead to self-fulfillment: healing our wounds by directly facing inner demons such as the *Judge* and *Victim.*

Chapter 10: Mastery of Intent 129

Here we see how life is lived when we traverse the "three clear paths." As Masters of Intent, we move beyond the realm of "problems" into the world of revelation and effortless manifestation.

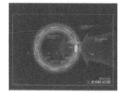

Chapter 11: Beyond Desire 137

Once again, an overview of the Human Form floating in the ocean of *Being*. Having moved beyond personal desires, our personal will has merged with that of the Universe; the miracle of Life simply flows through us.

Chapter 12: Return to Being 143

In this final map, the soul can melt back into the ocean of love, consciousness, and Being, or incarnate into another life on earth. To be or not to be, our choice; we are free.

PRACTICES 147

For Attunement to Being 148

For Detachment from Outcomes 153

For Healing the Wounds 158

ABOUT THE AUTHOR 165

FOREWORD

BY DON MIGUEL RUIZ

Author of The Four Agreements, Mastery of Love

Map of Desire is a truly unique tool for personal liberation. It consists of a series of diagrams of *inner landscapes*. When I first saw them, I was momentarily surprised, "What is this? And why does it seem to represent someone so unaware, so caught by the dream of the planet?" However, as more maps continued to unfold, I saw that they showed a *process*, the transformation of someone waking up from a dream of hell into a life of personal freedom. Like all maps, its great value was to show us where we are, how we got here, and how best to get where we really want to go.

Step-by-step through a series of beautiful, concise "blueprints," along with a selection of practical exercises, these maps will lead you to discover time-tested pathways to finding true peace and happiness. With this book, I deeply appreciate how the spiritual wisdom of Toltec masters is now available to the general public through the power of art.

Fu-Ding is unusually qualified to create this project. These blueprints bring together his background as an architect and artist with his devotion to express high spiritual insights. From years of experience in Eastern as well as Western spiritual practices, he has become one of the best Toltec teachers I know. He is a *nagual*, a Master. So study these maps, follow the guidance, and you will find yourself *enjoying* your journey towards new levels of self-fulfillment.

* * *

PREFACE
How To Use This Map

This map is a blueprint for self-fulfillment. It will show us why we don't get what we want, and how to identify and obtain what we truly want. But unlike a normal map, this is one of *inner* landscapes. It charts our psyche filled with topographical features like the location of heart, the territory of ego, and the headquarters of inner demons that sabotage from within.

Built on timeless wisdom from East and West, the ideas and practices presented here have been effective for years with individuals and groups. It has been continually inspiring to see how decades of debilitating attitudes can be transformed in just a few months of committed practice. All that is required is a few guidelines and trust in the natural wisdom of the heart.

How to use this map

This Map is best used by engaging yourself in two ways—through *reason* for the concepts discussed in the text, and through *intuition* and *imagination* for insights that the pictures, stories, and quotes may evoke. As you read, I encourage you to pause now and then for revelations to arise and for consciousness to shift. These pauses, simple as they may seem, can help fulfill one of the main purposes of this book— to awaken us to who we truly are.

> *"We are God. But we are dreaming*
> *that we're not. Wake up!"*
>
> —don Miguel Ruiz
> *(The Four Agreements)*

Of course no map in itself can decide for us what to do or where to go. But it can show us which roads are tortuous and which clear and direct so that we can make our own informed decisions. Even as we retain freedom of choice, then, we will be guided—shown where and how to blaze our own paths to self-fulfillment.

Since this *is* a **Map of Desire**, we begin by examining the nature of desires. Let's take a look at what happens when we want something.

Desires

Having a desire triggers a complex decision-making process that involves reason, feelings, judgments, and other components of our psyche. Ideally, if those thoughts, feelings and judgments are all aligned toward the same goal with no internal contradictions, we will have what the shamans call *Clarity of Intent*. The trajectory of our desire will be a straight, clear path to our goals—we see what we want, we go for it, and we get it...

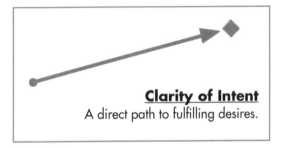

Clarity of Intent
A direct path to fulfilling desires.

But, alas, as seen in the drawing, most of the time the trajectory of our intent becomes contorted or blocked by obstacles of all kinds—physical, financial, social, psychological. Such blockages, as shown by the black diamond, invariably trigger complex psychological reactions filled with unresolved wounds, prejudices, fears, and sorrows—"distortions," as we call them—that keep us from reaching our goals.

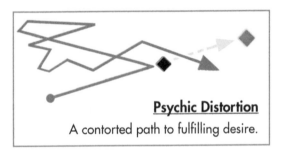

Psychic Distortion
A contorted path to fulfilling desire.

Contrast this with the first diagram that shows no obstacles or distortions at all because with Clarity of Intent, there is no judgment; what used to be considered an "obstacle" is seen to be part of the natural texture of life. Free of distortions, we can move easily towards our goals. But first things first—What *are* these distortions, and what can we do about them?

Distortions

Distortions are anything within our psyche that veers us off course from a straight, clear path to our goals. What causes them? Our own emotional, psychological and physical conditions. For example, *emotional* distortions can come from a wounded heart that was betrayed by a family member or loved one. Or they can be generated by an unfocused rage at the world that started with an abusive upbringing.

Psychological distortions can be caused by low self-esteem perhaps due to unrelenting criticism as a child or by too much hubris derived from deep insecurities. *Physical* sources of distortions include worries over weight problems, physical handicaps, chronic illnesses, or racial differences. To summarize, anything within our psyches that is not pure and balanced will cause distortions.

In our interactions with the world in all its complexities, our distortions quite often react accordingly and develop their own complexities in response. Anger, shame and judgments often flare. For instance, when we present a cherished project to the world and it is unceremoniously refused, our distortions can become more complicated, deepening our pain. Even positive feedback can cause our psyche to reverberate with complex reactions.

Our distortions are further complicated by the fact that we usually have dozens of desires (and their attendant distortions) going on at the same time. Typically, we want more meaningful sources of income, harmony in our relationships, relief from a chronic health problem, and a much-needed vacation…with each of these desires spawning many more. Given this situation, our combination of desires and distortions look as shown on the right…

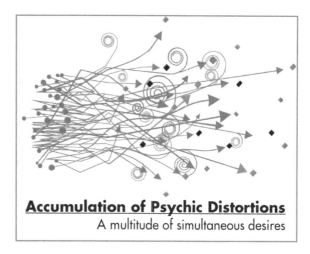

Accumulation of Psychic Distortions
A multitude of simultaneous desires

Placing this accumulation of psychic distortions on to our Map, we can see where these distortions occur in our psyche, as shown in the next drawing…

The accumulation of red arrows represents our plethora of desires. It shows the condition when our desires, primarily generated from ego, are confused, contradictory and chaotic. Feeling un-

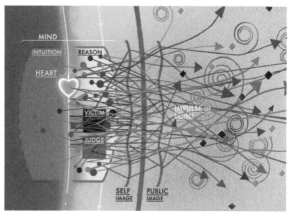

Tyranny of Desire
A psyche filled with desires and distortions.

fulfilled, our ego only knows to desire *more*, which only adds to the vicious cycle. Thus, focusing mainly on ego demands, we forget that what we truly want can come only through the heart.

This map of the **Tyranny of Desire** represents a condition that applies to the vast majority of us. Indeed, it applies to our society at large where conflict, contradictions and gridlock abound. It is not a pretty picture, but at least we have begun to face our predicament with eyes wide open.

The good news is that in spite of the tyranny of our desires, there is a way out. In beginning this book, we have already begun the process by assessing the reality of our situation. In shamanic terms, we have begun to cultivate the "Mastery of Awareness"—acknowledge *what is*—which is the essential first step to self-transformation. The Map does this by declaring with unblinking candor, *We are here*. In the following chapters, we will see *how* we got here, and *where* to find the best ways out to our personal freedom.

With the Map as our guide and techniques to transform distortions, we can now make real progress towards resolving our issues and fulfilling our original intent to know "why we don't get what we want and how to obtain what we truly want."

In the chapters that follow, all these issues and processes will be covered in detail. The Map is always here to provide visual references for your progress, and to remind you of your essential wholeness. We trust that as you go through the pages that follow, you will find inspired and practical ways to clear paths on your way to self-fulfillment and true happiness.

* * *

ACKNOWLEDGMENTS

Just as a flower depends on the support of soil, water, and sun to bloom, *Map of Desire* would not have blossomed without the support of invaluable friends and colleagues. First, I thank Spirit and guides seen and unseen for inspiration and advice from development to fruition.

On a human scale, immeasurable gratitude goes to my beloved friend, mentor, and shaman don Miguel Ruiz who woke me up to reality. With this awakening, I received new eyes that allowed this book to be conceived and developed. Deep thanks goes to Richard Strauss who gave invaluable feedback from conceptual stages to present, and who co-wrote the Illuminations in the book.

I honor the many friends and associates whose perceptions and candor helped knock off rough edges of the manuscript until it shone like a gem. They include Norman Kadarlan and Rafael Monserrate, both of whom read and re-read the manuscript bringing great insights all along the way. Deep gratitude goes to indelible inputs from Katya Williamson, Mehdi Davachi, Doraine Poretz, Steve Hasenberg, Adam Hall, Linda Jacobson, FuTung Cheng, Maija Wilder, Jeff Hutner, Art Ellis, Laurel Airica, and the many participants of my Shamanic Workshops over the years with whom ideas and maps were developed.

Profound thanks goes to all the poets, seers and sages whose insights and aphorisms have helped light up my life. Some have found their way into this manuscript, including two poems by Rumi brilliantly translated by Coleman Barks, and quotes from Carl Jung, don Miguel Ruiz, Sri Sai Baba, Maharishi Mahesh Yogi, Max Planck, William Blake, Walt Whitman, Lao Tzu, Rabindranath Tagore, Ralph Waldo Emerson, and Evans-Wentz's version of *The Tibetan Book of the Dead*.

Great appreciation goes to those who helped publish and market the manuscript including agent, author and friend, Bill Gladstone and Gayle Newhouse of Waterside Productions, Jeff Reznikoff for book design, and Pep Monserrate for general marketing and coordination of all my books, art and workshops.

* * *

INTRODUCTION

Maps have long fascinated human beings. They tell us where we are, where we've been, and where we are going. *Map of Desire*, however, is not an ordinary guide. It charts pathways through *inner* landscapes, tracks the trajectory of our aspirations and, ultimately, provides a working blueprint for personal fulfillment.

With so much of contemporary life in turmoil, how do we face and maneuver past our own fears? Jobs seem uncertain, loved ones feel distant, and dreams appear hopeless. So, what's the best course of action? Our formal institutions—religions, governments, and corporations—seem so removed from our personal well-being that many of us have sought to blaze our own unique paths towards self-fulfillment. But how do we start, what are the guidelines, where are the maps?

This book intends to answer those questions. Through a series of "maps," text, and true-life anecdotes, we'll find a candid assessment of how we came to our precarious predicament, and a blueprint that shows, step-by-step, the way from turmoil to transcendence From *desire* comes all creation. In spiritual and shamanic traditions throughout the world, it is said that Spirit's desire to know itself gave birth to the universe. And with it, we humans, whose desires fuel our every thought, word and deed.

These twelve blueprints map the natural law of creation—quite simply, how "thoughts take form." They reveal the most common road-blocks to enlightened action, and make plain that through *Attunement to Being*, *Detachment from Outcomes*, and *Healing the Wounds*, we will find the three clear, time-tested pathways to material and spiritual well-being.

A personal journey
Map of Desire conveys the archetypal journey of human transformation from unconscious beginnings, through disillusionment and confusion, to decisive steps on the path towards personal freedom.

My own life story followed this pattern. Tragic circumstances during childhood (in-law problems, foster homes, beatings, etc.) instilled in me such overwhelming despair and melancholy that by the time I was in college, I was unable to find a true reason to live and found myself sleeping sixteen hours a day. Desperate to escape my sorrows, I threw myself into my vocation as an architect and gained success. Still, no building, no matter how beautiful, could fill the hole in my own heart. A fresh perspective on life had to be found, or death would find me before my time.

Then, fortuitously, a path appeared that rang true and clear—meditation. For once, I shifted my gaze to the *inner* man. In time, this shift refocused the purpose of my life to that of a seeker, which in turn propelled me to journey from the heights of the Himalayas in Kashmir to the base of the Pyramid of the Moon in Mexico. Here, after twenty-five years immersed in wisdom traditions East and West, my spiritual aspirations were fulfilled in a ritual that changed my life forever.

In the midst of sixty apprentices, as guided by the Toltec shaman Don Miguel Ruiz, I "jumped to the sun," and became a living conduit of energy between heaven and earth. Powerful, mysterious energy penetrated me to the core—"the power of love" an inner voice said to me—as I lost consciousness. My life since then has never been the same.

Though it would take me years to assimilate that transcendent experience, I found myself freed from the endless chatter of my own mind, and released from the grim determination to achieve goals, or even to be "enlightened." Instead, an appreciation for the moment came into my life, and with it an unassailable feeling of lightness. Moving through my daily life as if it were a dream, I could see that my problematical past, my wonderful projects, all were nothing but illusion, ephemeral, and ultimately unreal.

Freed from the constraints of the visible world of form, I perceived a spiritual dimension that filled me with peace and joy. With nothing to prove, nothing to defend, no fears, and no attachments, a deep sense of awe seeped into all my perceptions. As a visual artist, I gained new eyes, and saw the intrinsic radiance in everything from a common street corner to a blade of grass. What magic in the mundane!

I told my teacher about this newfound euphoria, and he laughed, "Yes, it gets to a point where the only thing that keeps you going is your intent, just because you say so, with nothing left to justify. You are free."

With his encouragement, I began to conduct shamanic workshops, including a ground-breaking course at the North Carolina School of the Arts: "Shamanic Tools for the Film-maker." There, participants often commented on my diagrams and how they helped to clarify what otherwise could have remained abstract and inaccessible.

Power of pictures

Thus, a vision was born—to express, diagrammatically, pathways that plumb the depth of our own divinity. This has evolved into the book you have now before you: a series of blueprints for self-fulfillment. Ultimately, I hope they will show, as Don Miguel Ruiz often proclaimed, "We are God. But we dream that we're not. Wake up!"

My fascination with charts and diagrams revealed itself early on in grammar school when I became obsessed with drawing an illustrated map of our subject of study, the California missions. Since then, as an architect and production designer, I gained a deep appreciation for the concise and elegant "language" of blueprints that can make clear in two dimensions even the most complex structures and concepts. In a house, for example, there is a "floor plan," "electrical plan," and so on, that cumulatively allows a wide range of tradesman to read the architect's intention from overall vision to the most specific details. Likewise, these "maps," through a layering of simple diagrams, show cumulatively the miraculous interplay of heart, ego, body and mind within each of us. Once perceived, we can gain *clarity of intent* in fulfilling our desires.

Increasingly, our world thinks in pictures. Appealing directly to intuition and emotions, the power of images, as utilized here, helps to cast light directly on the fundamental questions of life, and illuminate a divine plan: to expand our consciousness so that we may rediscover our true nature, glorious beyond measure.

About this book

You will find four elements in these pages:

a. **Maps**

These blueprints reveal the *inner* landscape within each individual such as heart, mind, intuition, and ego. Like any map, it shows visually the *relationship* between these elements, how they interact, how they can be cultivated and/or sidestepped befitting our paths through life.

Furthermore, the series of twelve blueprints tell the story of our evolution over time beginning with our source in *Being*, the development of the miracle of our human form, and continuing to where we are now—facing the dire plight of our lives filled with violence, corruption and greed. No wonder many of us feel lost and confused and yearn for a way out of our predicament. Three of the maps fulfill that yearning by showing time-tested pathways out of our malaise, until finally, in the last three maps, we're shown clear trajectories of how our lives can be when filled with freedom and joyous creativity.

b. Text.

As a running commentary on the maps, the text brings clarity to the diagrams while highlighting fundamental principles relevant to self-fulfillment. Authentic anecdotes bring to life all topics discussed.

c. Illuminations.

Interspersed throughout the text are "Illuminations," mytho-poetic commentary on the text that embodies the emotional/psychological essence under discussion. Designed to appeal to one's imagination and intuition, they are highlighted by their placement in blue boxes.

d. Practices.

To gain-first hand *experience* of situations described in these chapters, we offer powerful exercises that have proven highly effective in workshops over the years. They relate directly to Chapters #7, #8, and #9 and their "three clear paths" towards self-fulfillment.

Awakening to our destiny

The maps, text and Illuminations altogether reveal a story fundamental to us all: that of awakening to our own destiny by knowing who we are. *Know thyself.* A tale filled with challenge and adventure, here is a brief overview of this noble quest:

Since the dawn of time, as revealed in the first three chapters, we humans have asked the fundamental questions: "Why are we here?" "Where did we come from?" And, "What lies ahead?" To throw light on these questions, we begin at the beginning by considering our source in *Being* and the mystery behind all things. From within *Being*, we see the first glimmerings of an individual soul, which in turn allows the creation of the human form with its miraculous instruments of consciousness, the human heart and mind. So equipped, our life begins.

The next three chapters confront us with a thorny question, "Given the wondrous body–mind–spirit that we are, and a beautiful, nurturing planet on which to live, why have we filled our lives with such anxiety, materialism and violence that has brought us to the brink of self-destruction? How did we become so lost and confused?

Though we might feel overwhelmed by the chaos of our times, we have, thanks to the wisdom of the ages, three clear pathways that can show us the way out from confusion towards personal freedom. The next three chapters clarify those pathways with explanations, guidance, and exercises. These Practices allow us to *experience* the peace and self-fulfillment inherent in our true nature.

Finally, having removed layer upon layer of delusions inside and out, we can stand in splendor having fulfilled our destiny by becoming awake to who we truly are. The last three chapters express this freedom, and the transcendent choices now open to us.

May the **Map of Desire** help your journey towards self-fulfillment be filled with adventure and joy.

* * *

PART ONE
OUR JOURNEY BEGINS

Since the dawn of time, we humans have asked the fundamental questions: "Why are we here?" "Where did we come from?" And, "What lies ahead?" These first three maps begin at the beginning by considering our source in the Mystery behind all things.

1. BEING

It was from the Nameless that
Heaven and Earth sprang.

—Lao Tze

Long before a beginning…Being is.

At first glance, this statement may give one pause. Why is it written, "Being is" rather than "Being was," which would be grammatically correct? Upon reflection, what appears to be an error is, in fact, accurate. Being is beyond time, has always existed, and always will. Being is, as the Buddhists say, "unmade, unborn, and unmanifest."

But before we go too far, the question arises: Why should we care? With all the responsibilities of daily life, especially in these tumultuous years, who has the time to explore such notions, sublime as they may be? How can Being help me pay my bills or deal with challenges in my relationships? Can it help me find peace in my troubled life?

The answer is an emphatic, YES! Why? Because in Being resides the resolution to all problems, all dreams, and all that we are. Being is synonymous with Love. If we can see beyond names and appearances, our world-view expands well beyond our ego's limited version of reality. and we see who we truly are, pure love. Bold as it may seem, it's something that most of us have experienced. For example, when you fall in love, whether you know it or not, you are attuning to Being, and suddenly, in spite of all mundane problems, life becomes miraculous beyond description. Being is beyond description.

Being is something to actively cultivate. In Chapter 7, we will delve into this more deeply, and under Practices at the end of the book, you will find step-by-step instructions to connect with Being. So, just as tributaries of all rivers somehow flow back to their source in the sea, all our desires for fulfillment, meaning, and love will eventually find their roots back in Being. To begin at the beginning, then, here's Map 1, ***Being***:

LEGEND • PART ONE : OUR JOURNEY BEGINS

Map 1: BEING

In the beginning...

Map 1, *Being*, portrays a field of pure space represented by the wide emptiness of the blueprint. Except for the borderline and labels, nothing is yet delineated because Being, although filled with consciousness, energy, and love, is free of all visible forms. Everything remains in potential.

This is the Source of the universe and everything in it, including all humans.

BEING

B E I N G

Beyond form

As can readily be seen in this first map, we have a blueprint with nothing in it. How appropriate, considering that *Being* is another way of saying the *Unmanifest*. It can be pictured as an infinite space filled with emptiness, a void of pure existence that is free of all limits of time, hence the phrase, "Long before a beginning…*Being* is." (A similar example of trying to express the infinite in spite of the limits of words can be found in the Bible when Jesus says, "Before Abraham was, I Am." The transcendent spiritual aspect of Jesus is beyond time.)

Long before a beginning…
Being is.

Though Being is completely formless, it nevertheless teems with energy and consciousness and serves as the ultimate unifying reality. As seers have declared since time immemorial, it is also synonymous with love. This is our Source, the beginning and end of who we are, pure Being, pure love.

In Eastern traditions, this ultimate reality is called *Nirvana*, the *Absolute,* or the *Void.* Meso-American shamanic schools call it *Intent, Nagual,* or *Black Light* because it is light that can't be seen. Since it is beyond all language and labels, some traditions call it the Nameless. Nevertheless, to be able to even speak about it, it has also been called Spirit, Love, God, All That Is…or Being.

However it is named, it is from this "nothingness" that the manifest universe comes to be beginning with *visible* light, which in turn gives birth to the suns and galaxies of the universe. Out of those billions of suns, one of them energizes our own planet, which in turn vitalizes all life forms on earth including humans.

On a human scale, Being brings all its unfathomable vitality, consciousness, and love into all we are and all we do. When we're able to tune into it *consciously*, all its power and glory flows into us with much greater force. Daily problems may dissolve through a sudden insight, or love long yearned for can suddenly burst out of *our own hearts!* The beauty of nature, the eyes of a newborn child, these are everyday examples of how we may experience Being as it is revealed in the world of form. Moments of such perception can often leave us in wonder.

Luckily, through the centuries, spiritual and shamanic masters have provided exercises to gain *experience* of this reality beyond mere concept. In the Toltec shamanic tradition, for example, there are practices to meditate on "the space between the atoms" or "the space between thoughts," or "on your own heart." (See *Practices* at the end of this book for specific instructions.) Inherent in our essence, the light and love of Being is our birthright, and these "maps" will guide us on our way to reclaim it.

In Map 1, as mentioned above, the blueprint exists although nothing as of yet is delineated. This expresses how Being exists even though nothing is manifested in visible form. At the same time, it serves as the essential ground for all forms to take place.

Energy
Being has three qualities. Though invisible and formless, it is filled with energy, consciousness, and love. We'll examine each of these in turn.

Being is energy. Imagine a portion of the Universe devoid of all forms. Although light completely permeates this area, it remains invisible until it can hit something that will reflect it in a way we can see. (This invisible energy is the "black light" described by the Toltec shamans.) As soon as the light *does* hit something, Presto! we then notice planets, suns, a galaxy, a mote of dust. Likewise with the mysterious void of Being. Though invisible, it is the source of the energy that creates the light that reveals the suns, planets and all living things.

> *Being is energy...*
> *A surge of power, born from the unmanifest*
> *A billion suns ablaze in an ocean of Mystery*
> *igniting life in us all.*

A sense of the infinite vitality of life with its unending flow of energy can be seen in those "time-lapse" shots in movies where hours of activity flicker by in seconds. We see, for example, thousands of people hustling through Grand Central Station in New York who disappear through a dozen escalators only to be replaced by thousands more in an endless rush of humanity. Or, perhaps, in other time-lapse shots, we see thousands of cars in an endless stream of freeway rush hour, or pictures of billion blades of new grass pushing out of the soil each spring. All that *chi*, all that life force energy! The unlimited force of Being energizes everything in life.

Though "energy contained in Being" may sound abstract, that which is powerful but invisible is something we experience all the time, as with electricity. No one has ever *seen* electricity (a stream of electrons), so, like Being, it remains invisible, yet we most certainly see its effects, and work with it constantly to benefit from its power.

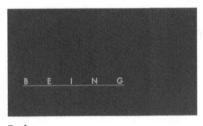

Being
Infinite potential in the unmanifest.

In Map 1, the manifestation of this energy from Being is still *in potential*. Nothing yet has materialized, therefore the map shows only an expanse of a blue background waiting for the first impulse of something to manifest.

Consciousness

Being is consciousness. Again, imagine an infinite space devoid of stars, planets or any form of celestial bodies. Though empty of visible form, it is filled not only with energy as described above, but also consciousness. Mystics, (and more recently cutting edge physicists) have long divined that the ultimate nature of reality lies in consciousness. In the shamanic tradition, this awareness that lies beyond words is called *silent knowledge*.

Once the universe did take form (and it remains a mystery as to why), this consciousness, this cosmic "intelligence" was transmitted through light, which pervaded everything in the universe. It established, for example, laws to maintain relationships between energy and matter, kept planets on their proper orbits, and produced and harmonized the complex organizing principles of natural law.

> *Being is consciousness...*
> *Pure emptiness, pregnant with silent knowledge.*
> *From galaxy to human, all destinies unfold*
> *Through the unfathomable intelligence of Being.*

On the scale of humans, this intelligence was able to provide volumes of information essential to our maintenance through a single cell of DNA, plants could know how to "eat light" for food through photosynthesis, birds could intuit just the right time to migrate, and we, complete with self-regulating organs and powers of perception, could not only function and enjoy this physical planet, but also exercise self-reflective awareness to fulfill our destinies of knowing who we truly are.

Nowadays, with accelerated change on every level of contemporary life, scientists have been blurring hard divisions between energy and matter (as well as between spiritual and material life). Furthermore, leading quantum physicists have begun to accept not only that all in Creation is but one form or another of energy (as with $E=mc^{2)}$), but also that all in the Universe is filled with "intelligence"—

> *"All matter originates and exists only by virtue of a force...*
> *We must assume behind this force the existence of a conscious*
> *and intelligent Mind. This Mind is the matrix of all matter."*
>
> —Max Planck, originator of Quantum Physics

This pronouncement aligns with that of the spiritual teacher Maharishi Mahesh Yogi. A life-long student of physics, he had conducted numerous experiments and symposiums with top scientists (including Nobel Prize winners), and used the language of our times—quantum physics—to help give credence to what he had always perceived:

"The universe is structured in consciousness."

—Maharishi Mahesh Yogi

In Map 1, the manifestation of this consciousness, as with energy, is still *in potential* so the blueprint still remains empty except for the expanse of the blue field.

Love

Being is love. Proclaimed by sages, seers, and poets the world over as the most powerful force in the Universe, love allows all aspects of Creation to interact in harmony. From proton to electron, man to woman, heaven to earth, all that exists commingles in love. From the beginning as young children, our natural tendency has always been to love.

Being, through the world of form, communicates its love with us all the time. When our perceptions are open to feel and experience what we experience (instead of letting *reason* explain them away because they may not be logical), we can feel the love aspect of Being all the time through Mother Nature. The warmth of the sun, the sound of creeks, the fragrance of wildflowers—all are Nature's manner of a loving embrace. For those more attuned, Being's continuous loving interaction with us keeps us alive with everything from bodily sensations to intuitive insights. If we're open, we may even find that we can communicate with animals, hear a rose tell us, "I love you" through the language of perfume, and express our love for nature simply by caressing her with our footsteps through the wilderness.

> *Being is love...*
> *Radiant wellspring, fulfillment of all desire.*
> *Proton and electron, man and woman, heaven and earth*
> *   all that exists commingles in love.*

Love is synonymous with Being. At this fundamental level of existence, the meaning of both these words transcends all limitation and merge into one. Both express the phenomena of a universal connector, the First Cause, the ultimate Source of all existence.

However, the word, "love" expresses this from the viewpoint of feeling, whereas "Being" describes it from the stance of the intellect. Both remain invisible until they find an object that can reflect its qualities—pet, person or planet—and then they burst into life in a way that we can all deeply feel.

Wisdom begins when we recognize that behind the visible world of our lives, there is the world of Being that is our radiant Source. From here, we can find the true fulfillment of all desires because this is the only reality beyond the ephemeral illusions of form that come and go. To recognize Being is to know that we are all, in essence, pure love, powerful, and imperishable. To gain this awareness is the *primary* purpose of our life on earth, a chance to expand our consciousness so that we know our oneness with Spirit.

> *I honor those who try*
> *to rid themselves of any lying,*
> *who empty the self*
> *and have only clear being there.*
>
> —Rumi

In Map 1, nothing, at this point, has yet materialized to love, so all remains as a possibility. Just as the formless void of *Being* is the invisible ground for all manifestation in form to occur, the empty blue field of this blueprint serves as the neutral background for all drawings to come.

* * *

2. ETHERIC BODY

The Sun has devoted one ray of light
to become you.

—don Miguel Ruiz

Given the vast ocean of mystery that is Being, how is that we exist with each of us a unique individual with our own thoughts, feelings and will? The answer lies with the etheric body, or the human soul. From within infinite Being, a mysterious impulse gives rise to a body made of the subtlest of matter, ether, which in turn serves as the groundwork that allows full development of the human form. The etheric body, then, is an essential link between the universality of infinite Being with the specificity of a single individual.

For many, such thoughts can boggle the mind. The good news is that ultimately, comprehension of these matters comes from feelings. Fundamental questions with answers beyond the reach of reason are resolved in our hearts. Like falling in love, these are not issues to understand, but rather feelings to experience.

I am so small I can barely be seen
How can this great love be inside me?
Look at your eyes. They are small,
But they see enormous things.

—Rumi

We *do* want to cultivate our hearts so that we can feel the truth of these matters. When we do, we find that there is nothing to learn, because we already embody love, soul and Being. We may have forgotten, but how we can once again remember is a primary purpose of our personal journey, and this book. Here, then, is the Map of the *Etheric Body...*

LEGEND · PART ONE : THE JOURNEY BEGINS

Map 2: ETHERIC BODY

The map of the Etheric Body shows a diaphanous
ring of light. Barely visible, it emerges from the field of infinite
space, and represents the first manifestation of
of an individual through the formation of the soul.

BEING

ETHERIC
BODY

BEING

ETHERIC
BODY

Entering the world of form

With the Etheric Body, we take the first step for us to become unique beings in the world of form. A profound question then arises: *Why?* If Being is pure love, as stated above, and we are already part of it, why would anyone consider leaving such perfection to become embroiled in the tumult of physical life?

> *Out of the Majesty,*
> *A spark of life,*
> *A primordial thought:*
> *I am that I am.*

Though this question has often been shrouded in mystery, mystics and sages through the centuries have divined that it was because, "Spirit desired to know Itself." This mandated a display of the infinite variety of forms, feelings and phantasmagoria inherent in Being. Otherwise, how would it know what it is if nothing whatsoever ever took form to be known? As a consequence, Being chose to express itself *in form*, and produced Mother Nature and the entire universe as a visible mirror of itself.

> *"Eternity is in love*
> *with the productions of time."*
>
> —William Blake

To know thyself

Likewise, on a human scale, *why we came to be* continues to be among the question of questions. And again, seers have repeatedly presented to us the answer: "To know thyself." This desire for self-realization—self-reflective conscious awareness—gave impetus to each of us to incarnate as a physical being on a physical planet such as earth. Consisting of hot and cold, good and evil, and all the opposites, life on earth allows us to know beyond mere concept our own true nature by letting us *experience* the full vastness of who we are from flesh to spirit, fear to love.

On a fundamental level, we exist, are consciously aware, and are in bliss. In Vedanta philosophy, a word that describes this basic reality of who we are is *satchitananda*. *Sat* means existence, *chit* means consciousness, and *ananda* means bliss.

> *From darkness to light...I am.*
> *That I exist, am aware, and in bliss...I am.*
> *But the "I" in I am...*
>   *Are we then separate from the One?*

To know that you are one with everyone, you must know separation and loneliness. To know you are perfect, you must experience imperfection. To know love, you must experience fear. To know from the viewpoint of Spirit that "I am that I am" (with no need whatsoever to justify your existence), you must experience a society whose expectations and conditions continually impose their values onto your lives. Through such situations, you can then taste the full possibilities of human experience so that you can know the richness of who you are.

Etheric Body
Manifesting the human soul.

In Map 2, the first sign of incarnation is seen with the *Etheric Body*, the formation of the Human Soul. Symbolically depicted as a translucent ring of light, it is the first manifestation of a human into the realm of form. As subtle as it is, it provides the electro-magnetic force field that will allow the complexities of the upcoming human form to unfold.

What's more, the Etheric Body contains the blueprint of our divine destiny. It holds the memory of the unfathomable wisdom of the Universe (or the *Akashic Records*," as Eastern mystics call it). When we develop our intuitive powers and receive powerful visions and insights, we are accessing the memory contained in our Etheric Bodies.

The soul takes form

Being (or Spirit) is, in essence, the same as the *Etheric Body*, (or soul) with the difference only in emphasis. Whereas the word "spirit" expresses the *concept* of this reality, "soul" suggests its *feeling* tone (for instance, "I was so moved by that soulful music..."). Whereas "spirit" conveys the vast transcendent, impersonal nature of reality, "soul" suggests the personal portion of infinity associated with a single person.

In a similar fashion, you could refer to a bedroom or a workspace in a house as "my" space, yet, with a window open, it is obvious that it merges with the openness outside, which in turn, is connected to the wide open spaces of earth, not to mention the heavens of outer space. Still, the term "my" space is convenient to bring the unlimited concept down to a human scale of everyday usage.

With the Etheric Body, you take the first step to wean yourself from your Source in Being to become an individual in a physical world. With your own personality and free will, your destiny is to become consciously aware that even as an individual, you reflect the whole of infinity.

In Map 2, the ring of light representing the *Etheric Body* has a soft edge that blends seamlessly into the blue color field. This expresses how the essence of the emerging individual soul is still (and always will remain) part of the infinite ground of *Being*.

> *Seeking to know oneself amidst infinity...*
> *A desire takes form.*
> *An elusive impulse ripples the ocean of Being*
> *and a soul is born.*

* * *

3. THE HUMAN FORM

The human body is the best picture
of the human soul.

—Ludwig Wittgenstein

In this chapter, we continue to track how the complex biological machine, the "human form," is built upon the foundation of the Etheric Body of the preceding chapter. Inspired by sacred diagrams of Eastern and Western wisdom traditions, we present the human being as a series of "sheaths" or bodies that reside one within the other. As we build upon the most subtle Etheric Body, layers of increasing density manifest in the form of the Emotional, Mental, and finally, Physical Body, the most solid of our sheaths.

An essential aspect to the Human Form is the miraculous instrument of consciousness, the Human Mind. (In the Map, the curved rectangular shape colored half yellow and half purple.) It allows us the ability to think and feel, to intuit and imagine, and to interpret the infinite stimuli we continuously gather with our five senses.

Finally, there is our Heart, strategically located to oversee everything from feelings to thoughts, from the spiritual to the physical. By knowing the unique role of each of the elements of our body and mind, how they interact, and what to "feed" them to keep them happy and healthy, we'll go a long way towards achieving clarity on how to make ourselves happy in all dimensions. Here, then, is Map 3, *The Human Form...*

LEGEND · PART ONE : THE JOURNEY BEGINS

Map 3: THE HUMAN FORM

Map 3, *The Human Form* displays a series of concentric circles that lie on top of a diaphanous ring of light. From inside out, these rings are shown as a red dotted, a black and yellow dashed, and a solid brown line that represent, respectively, the *Emotional, Mental and Physical Bodies* of the Human Form. They also define the *Interior and Exterior World* of the individual.

Between the Emotional and Mental bodies lies a curved rectangular shape colored half yellow and half purple that symbolizes an instrument of consciousness, the human *Mind*. The purple half, labeled *Intuition*, faces the interior of the individual, and the yellow half, *Reason*, faces the exterior world. Resting on the Emotional Body and strategically overlooking both sides of the Mind reigns the glowing symbol of the human *Heart*.

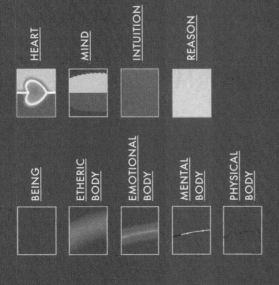

HEART

MIND

INTUITION

REASON

BEING

ETHERIC BODY

EMOTIONAL BODY

MENTAL BODY

PHYSICAL BODY

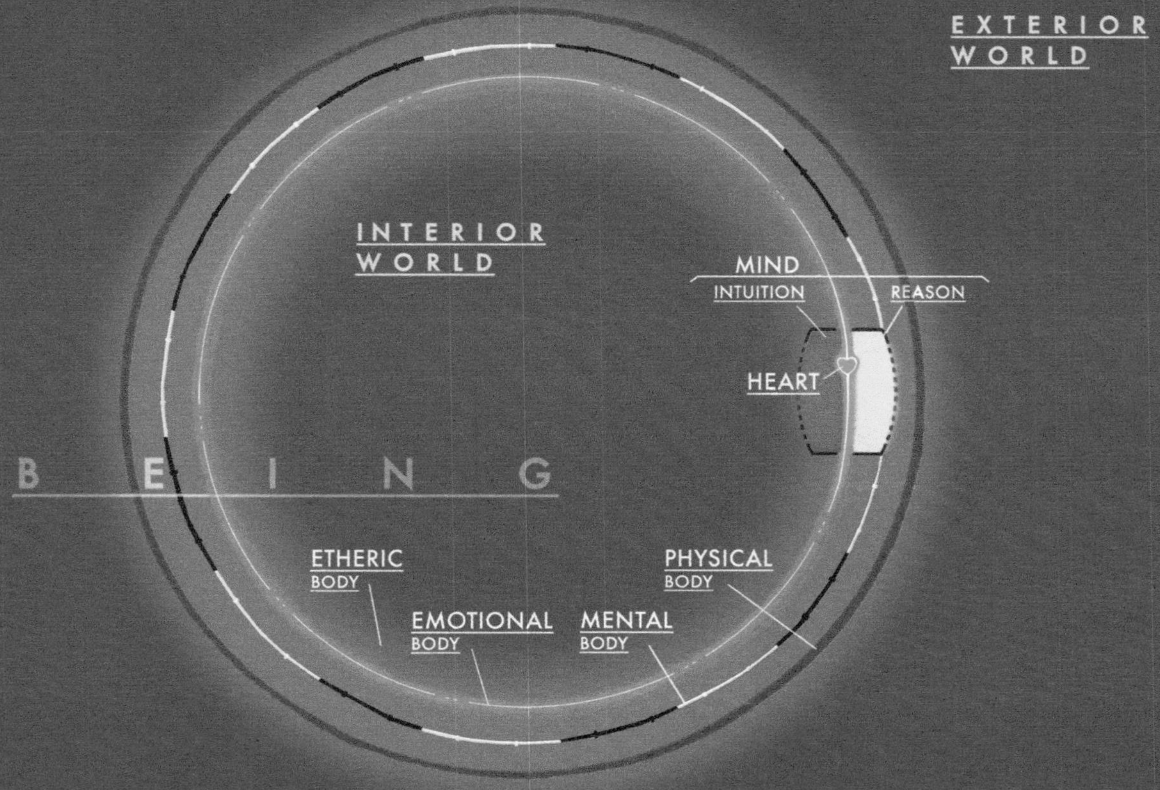
EXTERIOR
WORLD
INTERIOR
WORLD
MIND
INTUITION
REASON
HEART
BEING
ETHERIC
BODY
EMOTIONAL
BODY
MENTAL
BODY
PHYSICAL
BODY

MAP OF DESIRE

3. THE HUMAN FORM

> *With the breath of life*
> *Spirit enters matter*
> *And once again*
> *   the miracle unfolds...*

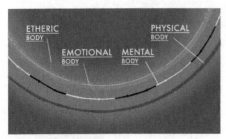

The Four Bodies
Layers of the human form.

The Human Form

To understand the role of each of the sheaths mentioned above, we'll again begin with the diaphanous white ring representing the subtlest of the four sheaths, the Etheric Body. It provides the foundation for the three subsequent rings.

The next layer less subtle, shown as a dotted line with a red glow, represents the *Emotional Body,* which gives us the capacity to *feel*. Since the subtle nature of feelings allows the most direct access to *Being,* it is situated in the innermost circle facing the *Interior World*. (Although *Being* is everywhere, it is best perceived by looking within into the *Interior World* due to the overwhelming distractions of daily life.)

> *"Feeling will get you closer to the truth of*
> *who you are than thinking."*
>
> —Eckhart Tolle

The next layer in increased density is the *Mental Body,* which gives one the power to *think*. This is depicted by a dashed black and yellow line in the map. The Mental Body allows the use of language, analysis, and interaction with the world. It will soon set up an ego structure to formulate self-identity, and systems of belief. With it come powers of discernment between truth and illusion, judgment and conscience, culture and art.

The final and most dense layer of the Human Form is the *Physical Body*, which serves as a "vehicle" so that our spirit can live in a material realm. In the map, this is shown as a solid, brown line. Equipped with five senses, the physical body is able to perceive through sensations much of the infinite qualities of the physical world, self-regulate its own internal organs, monitor its metabolism, and reproduce.

> *Body said to Soul: "If not for me*
> *You would have no place to live."*
> *Mind then replied: "Yet only through me*
> *Can you know how you think and feel."*
> *But Soul said naught,*
> *Knowing that through her, and her alone*
> *had they both come to be.*

Though the function of the physical body has often been described as a "container" for the soul to exist in a material world—"Take care of your body; otherwise, where will you live?" says a Zen proverb—this observation is true only from the viewpoint of the physical realm.

From the viewpoint of the spiritual, the etheric body actually "contains" the body, (opposite of what was stated above). The etheric body provides an electro-magnetic force field so that physicality can take form. This force field envelopes and permeates every cell of the body to sustain its life by feeding the energy and "intelligence" of Being into every cell, thus allowing the body to grow, self-regulate, and reproduce as it plays its part for the whole. Seen this way, the soul "contains" the body. Both of these observations, apparently contradictory, are true, depending on one's point of view.

In any case, in no way is the body a static container. Rather, it is charged with its own consciousness so it can grow, heal, and interact dynamically with all the other cells and organs, and still respond to elements as subtle as thoughts and emotions. It is truly a biological miracle, our Human Form.

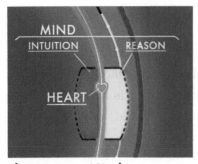

The Human Mind
Instrument of consciousness.

To *operate* this body, there is the instrument of consciousness, the Human Mind. In the map, it is indicated by the curved rectangular shape, half violet and half yellow, which represents the two distinct "software programs" utilized for us to live on earth:

Intuition: The purple side of the mind represents *Intuition* and *Imagination*. They allow us to tap into the infinite powers of the universe through insights, dreams, and visions. Through these software programs, we gain direct access to All That Is.

Reason: The yellow side of the mind represents the *Intellect* and *Reason*. These programs allow us the powers to analyze and use language, essential to the exterior world dominated by linear time and space, family and society.

Thanks to these two modes of operation, we can function in both worlds of Spirit and form, the eternal and the time-bound, heaven and earth.

> *Intuition now declared her gifts:*
> *"I attune you to true worth,*
> *Seduce you with wonders of heaven*
> *   and inspire genius for your life on earth."*

> *Of course, Logic and Reason had to have their say:*
> *"We set boundaries—time, language, and form.*
> *Impressions of knowledge and order*
> *   now have the means to be born."*

In this Map 3, we find located in the center of both sides of the mind and resting directly on the *Emotional Body* the glowing symbol of the *Heart*. Strategically situated at the epicenter of the Human Form, it has the unique ability to access and unify the spiritual, emotional, mental, and physical bodies.

The Human Heart
The great unifier.

This strategic positioning of the heart can also be seen in the Eastern system of power centers called *chakras* with the Heart chakra situated in the center between three lower ones (dealing with physical life), and three upper ones (dealing with the spiritual).

With a pure and open heart central to your being, you are now ready to be born and meet the rough and tumble world filled with adversity and challenges. Because your pristine heart is so accommodating as to provide love with no conditions, more often than not it will suffer physical, psychological, and emotional wounding. (Much more on this later.) With each us a hologram of the whole, we are each re-enacting the Biblical fall from grace. But why?

The answer is the same as we had discussed before, to *know thyself*. Only through the dramas of life that continually bounce us between heaven and hell can we fulfill the promise *through experience* of realizing, eventually, that we are much more than all our trials and triumphs put together.

> *The Heart listened well...*
> *Crossroads of all that is sacred and vile*
> *Keeping its secrets unspoiled*
> *by cruel innocence or guile.*

As the process unfolded, you started to develop "secondary purposes" of your life—cultivating minds, careers, and relationships—as a way to fulfill your "primary purpose" of knowing the richness and depth of who you truly are. Thus, from the viewpoint of self-realization, you could say to yourself, "bring on the trauma, the triumphs, the rush to conclusions…"

Through the wounding, and its healing (which we will delve into more detail in Chapters 7, 8, and 9), we *do* transform and eventually see that, yes indeed, we are more than our desires and possessions, laughter and tears. We *can* rise up like the phoenix from the ashes of our own ignorance with full awareness of our true nature. Such is the promise of the challenges of life we are all destined to face.

Map 3, *The Human Form,* at this point depicts a human being fully equipped in body, heart and mind, ready to be born into the complexities of physical life. You'll notice that the character of the line-work of the various bodies express the qualities they represent:

- The diaphanous ring of light of the Etheric Body on which all the other bodies rest, represents the all-pervading, indefinable quality of the soul.
- The line of the Emotional Body glows red with no distinct edge showing how emotions tend to radiate and flow freely with no clear border.
- The line of the Mental Body is dashed yellow–black, yellow–black to denote the nature of the mind that organizes, defines, and analyzes.
- The line of the Physical Body is brown and solid to convey the concrete quality of physical matter.

With body, mind and Spirit all in place and ready to play their proper roles, we enter Part Two, which will reveal to us what happens as we plunge into the great adventure of life in the material world. We're ready to be born.

> *Bring on the trauma, the triumphs, the rush to conclusions*
> *The courage, cowardice, ecstasy, and tears!*
> *Welcome the folly, the phantasmal delusion,*
>   *demons among angels, love laced with fears.*

* * *

PART TWO
<u>LOST AND CONFUSED</u>

Given a beautiful, nurturing planet in which to live, and the miracle of our body–mind–spirit, why are our lives filled with anxiety, fear and violence? What has brought us to the brink of self-destruction? How did we become so lost and confused?

4. CHALLENGES OF LIFE

Life is a challenge, meet it!

Life is a dream, realize it!

Life is a game, play it!

Life is Love, enjoy it!

—Sri Sai Baba

From the moment we are born, we're inundated with the overwhelming onslaught of strange faces, delights, wonders, and incomprehensible utterances coming at us urging us to do… something. But what? Just to be alive in this world requires a courageous sense of adventure. How do we cope?

Thanks to Mother Nature, we have instinct, a comprehensive "operator's manual" encoded in our DNA so that thousands of decisions are made automatically. As children, then, we are at one with nature. We live in the moment, play, and see the entire world as a giant toy to explore. We are innocent, pure, joyful…and unconscious.

Destiny, however, has higher aspirations for us—to become consciously aware of who we truly are. From the beginning, then, through parents, media, and schooling, we were weaned away from natural instinct in order to find our place in society through education, raising families, and launching careers. Thus began the life-long balancing act between natural instincts and the demands of society. Through our choices, and the trials and triumphs of life, the promise is that we will eventually transcend all disharmony, and find ourselves free. This is our destiny, our primary cause—to know who we truly are.

To fulfill this promise, we must first embrace the adventure of life. Through those trials and triumphs, we will know ourselves the only way we can, through experience. Here, then, is Map 4, *Challenges of Life…*

LEGEND · PART TWO : LOST & CONFUSED

Map 4: CHALLENGES OF LIFE

Map 4, *Challenges of Life* shows a close-up of the strategic area of *Heart* and *Mind*. The giant white arrow entering from the right represents the onslaught of the challenges of life that flow unceasingly from the world to the individual. Resting on the line of the *Emotional Body*, the *Heart* is poised strategically in the center of the *Mind* between *Intuition* and *Reason*.

The red arrows express an individual's desires and reactions in response to life's challenges. In the early years of childhood as represented in this map, these desires spring predominantly from the *Physical* and *Emotional Bodies* as *instinctual* desires. The black diamond, labeled *Obstacle*, represents a blockage on the path to the *Object of Desire*, which distorts the trajectory of the red arrow such that it never reaches its objective. This distorted arrow is labeled, *Reaction to Outcome.*

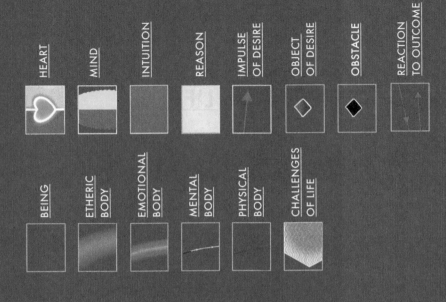

BEING

ETHERIC BODY

EMOTIONAL BODY

MENTAL BODY

PHYSICAL BODY

CHALLENGES OF LIFE

HEART

MIND

INTUITION

REASON

IMPULSE OF DESIRE

OBJECT OF DESIRE

OBSTACLE

REACTION TO OUTCOME

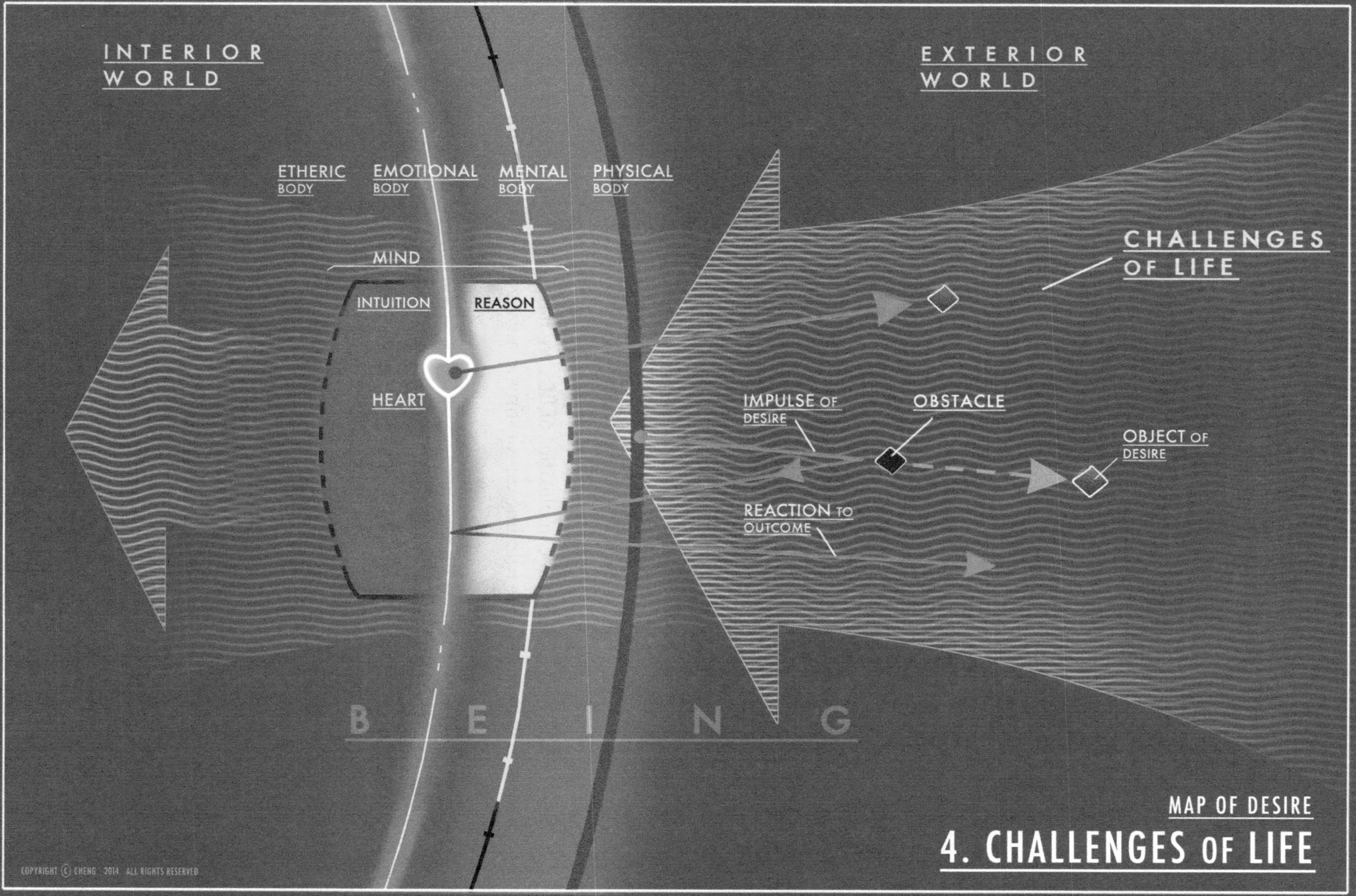

MAP OF DESIRE

4. CHALLENGES OF LIFE

CHALLENGES OF LIFE

EXTERIOR WORLD

OBJECT OF DESIRE

OBSTACLE

IMPULSE OF DESIRE

REACTION TO OUTCOME

INTERIOR WORLD

BEING

PHYSICAL BODY

MENTAL BODY

EMOTIONAL BODY

ETHERIC BODY

REASON

MIND

INTUITION

HEART

Challenges of life

To fulfill our destiny and expand consciousness, we are forced out of the warm, loving tranquility of the womb and immersed in the chaos and noise of life. To know how perfect we are, we have to experience imperfection to have something with which to compare. To know we are at one with "All That Is," we have to experience separation and individualism, and with it, loneliness, pride and fear. We are forced to bite the proverbial apple from the Tree of Knowledge, fall from our blissful state of grace to plunge into a world filled with problems, danger, and the complexities of opposites. Hot and cold, love and hate, "good and bad" become our daily bread.

> *Challenges of life*
> *Sure as ice, as fire*
> *Forge tragedy and triumph,*
> *and the world of desire.*

Seen this way, the biblical "fall from grace" in the Garden of Eden is not a curse (as Christianity generally stresses), but a blessing, an expansion, an opportunity to exercise our free will. Because of the rich complexities of life, we have many choices to make, each a chance to help us towards fulfilling our destiny to awaken to our true nature.

Instinctual desires

With the challenges of life so alluring, all you can do as an infant is to respond automatically and instinctively to the perplexing ocean of sights and sounds. With wide, open eyes you try to absorb everything. With intellect undeveloped, you can only gurgle or cry when you're hungry or cold. These yearnings rooted in nature and free of your conscious control are *instinctual desires*. Instinctively, your natural tendency is to live totally in the present, wonder, explore and play.

By the time you reach kindergarten the challenges of life compared to your infancy has expanded exponentially. With mental and psychological demands from family, school, and peers coming at you relentlessly, you soak in what you are taught, and imitate what you see. Being young and innocent, you have little perspective on the veracity of what you are told, and simply drink it all in. From the natural, safe, blissful but *unconscious* tendencies of childhood, you are thrown into the challenges of a problematical society.

> *"All psychic processes whose energies are not under conscious control are instinctive. Instincts in their original strength can render social adaptation almost impossible."*
>
> — Carl Jung

You are compelled to suppress your natural instinct if you are to avoid punishment and find your place in society. Early on, you learned to refrain from throwing tantrums in public places, respect authority, and manage your own fears in face of peers.

As more and more experiences become assimilated, you begin to refine your sense of self-identity. Through parenting and schooling, you develop habits and systems of beliefs, which for the most part, prove essential for survival in your community.

However, along with your parents' and teachers' positive guidance, you swallow whole-sale their prejudices, judgments, and for many, emotional and psychological abuse. As children new to the game of life, you assume that what you are told is true, and constantly try to adapt to survive. The abuse you may suffer is assumed to be a part of life, but, of course, it's not. *How* you adapt to these psychological wounds can often create patterns of behavior, which, unbeknownst to you, will secretly cause suffering for decades, if not your entire life. The challenges of life have just deepened greatly.

For example, a woman I know blamed her own son for all the terrible sufferings she had endured from her in-laws. She repeatedly beat him as a child and forced him to scrub floors while she insulted and kicked him. From the son's viewpoint, however, he never thought that this was "wrong," nor did he hate her, since he never had another mother with which to compare. It was "normal life," just something he had to learn to deal with. He *did* feel terrified around her, and developed a pattern of deep mistrust of adult women until well into his forties when, finally, he attained insight through therapy.

When as children our independent thinking begins to develop and we notice contradictions, injustice, and falsities—*"Why am I forced to go somewhere I don't want to go? Why was I yelled at for something I didn't do?"*—the first inkling of doubt and judgment takes root. If we rebel, punishments and rewards bring us back into line. Gone forever is the unconscious bliss of childhood. Confronting such complex situations, we are obliged to evaluate, choose, risk, fail and triumph, all of which expand and deepen our consciousness.

> *Impulsive and wild, we'd ravish and play*
> *How then could we deal with demands of the day?*
> *Domesticate, self-regulate and suppress primal fire?*
> *No matter our bent*
> *   will the world have its way?*

Between instinct and culture

These challenges are part of the struggle that Jung had mentioned above between our *instinct* (tied to nature) and *culture* (tied to social adaptation). Through this social adaptation, we cultivate loving relationships and careers. However, our challenges become exponentially more difficult when we begin to realize that society's behavior… borders on madness. (What other species on earth would pollute its own nest to the point of self-destruction, or amass enough bombs to annihilate itself many times over?) Torn between our natural instincts and society's demands, we become unfulfilled.

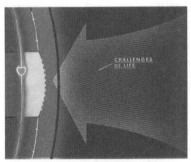

Challenges of Life
Unrelenting onslaught of the world.

A way out of this predicament is to withdraw our attention from the outside world and look within. To regain peace in the world, find the peace within. This process will be discussed in detail in upcoming chapters.

In Map 4, the size of the giant white arrow represents the magnitude of challenges that confront us from childhood onward through our entire lives. From parents to peer pressures, from economic upheavals to social injustice, the giant white arrow symbolizes the ever-changing complexities of life we are destined to confront.

Objects of desire.

As you develop, you obey the ways of the world and conform to the notion that the measure of "success" depends on your ability to manifest your objects of desire—that toy, that dress, that bike, and, as you mature, that diploma, that woman, that income.

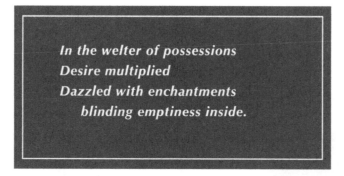

> *In the welter of possessions*
> *Desire multiplied*
> *Dazzled with enchantments*
> *   blinding emptiness inside.*

Up to a point, the aspirations for such "success" serve us well. As children, for instance, the gold star we received for our homework proved to be a wonderful incentive for future assignments. They helped us to focus our attention, learn the power of will, gain self-confidence, and experience the joy of work and accomplishment. For most people, this pattern of gaining fulfillment from the outside world is assumed to be a self-evident template for their entire lives even if, ultimately, they find it unfulfilling.

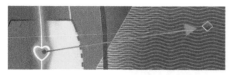

Instinctual Desires
Basic yearnings in line with nature.

In Map 4, representing our early stage in life as children, the thick, red arrows—one's instinctual desires—launch from the *Emotional* and/or *Physical Bodies* (from the Heart, in this case) None spring out of the Mental Body for the powers of the intellect have barely been awakened.

Discovery of the mind

Soaking in life like sponges with all our five senses when we were children, everything was a wonder. The world was ours to explore. But almost immediately, we were swept up in a whirlwind of demands and seductions, rewards and punishments. We were being groomed to be good citizens of society.

Encouraged by parents, media, and peers, we became educated, which meant for the most part to be rational and practical. *Reason* helped us cut through fogs of uncertainty as we made our plans, balanced budgets, and even tasted a bit of freedom and power from thinking for ourselves.

Education is power. After all, so we are taught, isn't it through the intellect and reason that science and technology, government and law came into existence? Inspired by stories of those who successfully made a difference, we began to foster our own ideas to contribute into the mix. We began to cultivate our minds in earnest as a way towards future success.

In Map 4, the red arrow, *Impulse of Desire* meets some obstruction as symbolized by the black diamond labeled, *Obstacle*. This obstruction could be any form of a set back or impasse, which invariably instigates a complex response within our psyche. This distorted arrow is labeled, *Reaction to Outcome*, and its trajectory can be seen bouncing back to the Emotional Body, and bouncing yet again to pass through the yellow area of reason, and then back out into the world. Whether our desires are fulfilled or thwarted, a complex reaction is typically triggered within our psyche, although the "Bounce-Back" shown here is relatively minimal and direct since the intellect has only just begun to be developed. For this same reason, no red arrows of desire spring from the dashed line of the *Mental Body* or the yellow area of *Reason*.

Reaction to Outcome
Complexity of psychological responses.

> *To know the One... savor the many,*
> *To know perfection... admit the imperfect,*
> *To know freedom of love,*
>   *embrace the bonds of fear.*

* * *

5. FORMATION OF EGO

A healthy ego must first be developed
before it can be transcended.

Anyone who has taken even a few steps on the spiritual path has come across the debilitating dangers of… ego. Oh, how we've been warned against its self-centered illusions that lie at the root of so much of our sorrows and heartaches.

And yet, we had to first develop an ego if we wanted to survive and find our place in the world. So, from a very young age, we were taught our names, what we could and couldn't do, and the dictates of society. Quickly, we were able to declare *my* family, *my* country, *my* opinions, and *my* dreams, and taught to reason, make judgments, and formulate an ego. So trained, we were able to function reasonably well in society.

But, as we reach maturity, many of us begin to feel unfulfilled and unhappy. "The problem is ego," proclaim the sages. Though many accept this to be true, why is it so difficult to overcome? The answer: We haven't yet distinguished that part of ego essential to our lives from that part which has become tyrannical. Until that distinction is made, we instinctively cling to our ego to avoid throwing the baby out with the bathwater.

Beneficial and essential characteristics of ego include a self-identity that allows us to function in society, and powers of discernment to distinguish between truth and illusions. On the other hand, some of ego's tyrannical qualities must be thrown off if we ever want to be truly happy, like arrogance, judgment, and self-importance. To show the principle elements of ego and its promises and perils, here is Map 5, *Formation of Ego*. Only by first knowing its blessings can we transcend its pitfalls…

LEGEND · PART TWO : LOST & CONFUSED

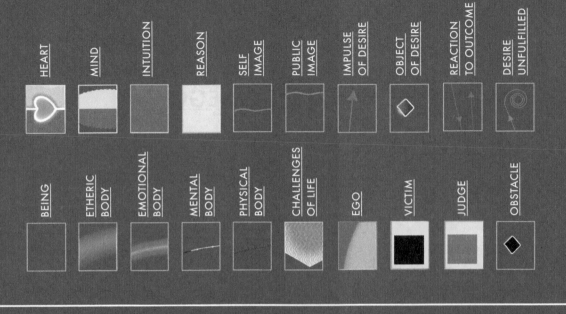

HEART

MIND

INTUITION

REASON

SELF IMAGE

PUBLIC IMAGE

IMPULSE OF DESIRE

OBJECT OF DESIRE

REACTION TO OUTCOME

DESIRE UNFULFILLED

BEING

ETHERIC BODY

EMOTIONAL BODY

MENTAL BODY

PHYSICAL BODY

CHALLENGES OF LIFE

EGO

VICTIM

JUDGE

OBSTACLE

Map 5: FORMATION OF EGO

Map 5, *Formation of Ego* diagrams further development of the Mind as it meets the ever-growing challenges of life. The large yellow-orange oval dominating the map depicts the *Ego* and its territory of control. Within the yellow portion of the Mind labeled, *Reason*, we find two squares, one red and one black, representing a *Judge* and a *Victim*, respectively. On both sides of the brown line of the *Physical Body* are two wavy green ones of *Self-Image* and *Public Image* that monitor interactions between the ego and the *Interior and Exterior World*.

The red arrow, *Impulse of Desire*, launches from the yellow area of *Reason*, but before it can reach its goal, it has met an *Obstacle* (the black diamond on the Map). This obstacle repels the arrow back, and instigates a complex trajectory as the arrow "bounces–back" between various components of the *Ego*. Labeled *Reaction to Outcome*, this portion of the red arrow ends in a red spiral representing a desire unfulfilled.

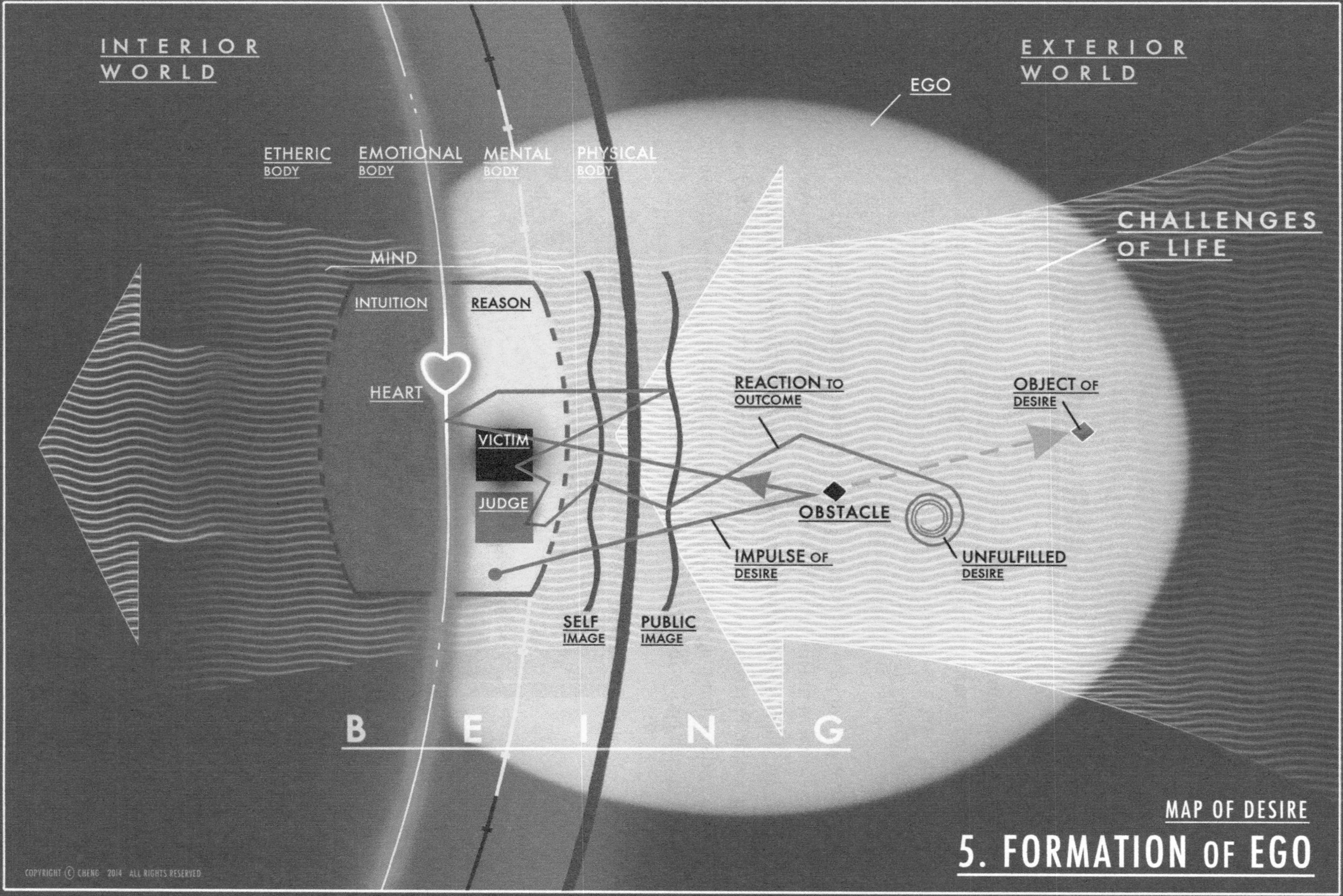

INTERIOR WORLD

EXTERIOR WORLD

CHALLENGES OF LIFE

EGO

OBJECT OF DESIRE

UNFULFILLED DESIRE

REACTION TO OUTCOME

OBSTACLE

IMPULSE OF DESIRE

PUBLIC IMAGE

SELF IMAGE

PHYSICAL BODY

MENTAL BODY

EMOTIONAL BODY

ETHERIC BODY

REASON

MIND

INTUITION

HEART

VICTIM

JUDGE

B E I N G

MAP OF DESIRE

5. FORMATION OF EGO

> *When, but a child*
> *We learn our name...*
> *ego is born.*

What is the ego?

To seriously explore the pros and cons of ego, the first question that arises is, *What is it?* As Carl Jung has stated, *"the ego is a mind-created complex of ideas from which we constitute our self–identity."*

With ego, you gain self-identity, and the miracle of becoming conscious of yourself as an individual in the midst of the vast continuum of life. Though your essence is eternal and infinite, thanks to ego, you can experience the richness of time and the intimacy of the particular. Furthermore, a fundamental aspect of the "mind-created complex of ideas" depends on language, which allows communication and self-expression. *Self-expression?* Thanks to ego, you have a "self" to express.

> *Out of the formless flow of life*
> *The miracle of identity!*
> *Each enters their story in the midst of its telling,*
> *a sovereign, original, Self-seeking entity.*

Formation of the ego

During childhood years as the ego first develops, it is so impressionable that whatever input you receive is absorbed wholesale. These first impressions, right or wrong, can often shape you the rest of your life. Though much in self-transformational books talk about the problems of the ego, as well they should, in itself there is nothing wrong with the ego. There are evolved and unevolved egos. With the proper upbringing, it could be nurtured into one that is balanced and healthy.

64

For example, a daughter of a friend whom I'll call Alicia lost her mother when she was ten. She was grief-stricken and at that young age had difficulty finding words for what she was going through. Many families that are insensitive to feelings about loss and death may be incapable of helping Alicia at all, or even berate her for being too moody or sensitive. This might leave the child's psyche scarred permanently with feelings of abandonment, rejection or guilt.

However, in my friend's case, he would take Alicia on long walks to dinner at night. It became an informal ritual that allowed Alicia to slowly at her own pace come out with subtle thoughts of what was disturbing her. Besides the grief over her mother, she had also begun to feel alienated from her schoolmates—she was an outsider, a freak, the "one with no mother."

Listening carefully, her father could then dispel the potential wound to her self-identity by first empathizing with her, "It must feel terrible to be an outsider." Alicia relaxed considerably. Then he suggested that maybe she was making an assumption, that she had no idea what was really going on inside each of her schoolmates. Perhaps others had lost family members, or were enduring poverty, or were even being abused, who knows? "For all we know, they all feel like an outsider," he told her. "Or perhaps your classmates envy *you* since you are always so friendly, popular and bright. What's more, what's wrong with feeling an outsider? Aren't most innovators, artists and pioneers with their independent minds considered outsiders?"

By such conversations, Alicia gradually regained her balance. Instead of this adversity traumatizing her unnecessarily, she actually gained wisdom of making "no assumptions" and to see behind the surface of things. Back on center, she excelled in her schoolwork, and with her father's guidance cultivated her mind *and* her character. Eventually, she won a full scholarship to an Ivy League college of her choice..

This story is an example of how the ego could be properly nurtured. However, in the vast majority of cases, this does not happen. The self-identity (ego) of the parents may be problematical from the start, so it's difficult to be balanced with the children.

Ego, as mentioned above, has many attributes essential for our survival—personal will, self-identity, self-expression. Why, then do so many sages and seers counsel against its formidable dangers? The definition from Jung as stated above helps throw light on this quandary: Ego, as our self-identity, depends on a *mind-created complex of ideas*. Ideas are generated from our thinking mind. We accept who we are according to what our thinking mind says we are, even though the greater part of who we are lies *beyond* our thinking mind—feelings, inner peace, love, dreams, happiness, intuition, imagination.

Although these qualities are not quantifiable, our mind-created ego still tries to crowbar them within the limits of reason. As a result, we feel obligated to justify our feelings, or explain away intuitive visions. Or simply ignore any experience that doesn't fit within the parameters of reason. If, for instance, we felt like becoming an artist, our ego might explain it away, "Be logical. What do *you* have to say that's so important? Anyway, you'll never make a living with it?" Reason can't be bothered about how fulfilling art can make us feel or how it feeds our soul.

If the shortcomings of ego and reason are so obvious, why does everyone in the world seem to revere them, and categorically dismiss feelings, dreams and intuition? ("Stop being so emotional. Be reasonable!") This is because the "complex of ideas" fits in perfectly with the tendency in our society to worship reason, logic, and their offspring: technology, science, facts, statistics…and ego. They don't consider the pain and suffering that this same "technology, science and facts" can produce with high-tech wars, stock-market manipulation, and entertainment filled with mindless violence. Things have become out of balance.

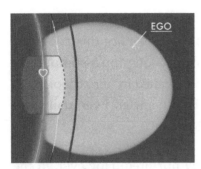

Territory of Ego
Self-identity according to reason.

In Map 5, the large yellow-orange oval labeled *Ego* dominates the graphic. This represents an individual beholden to the ego's idea of self-identity, a viewpoint of the vast majority of people. Within this yellow-orange territory, the bright yellow area, *Reason*, presides as if from headquarters over the territory of its creation, the ego.

Reason

One of the primary functions of *reason*, in the words of shamanic masters, is to monitor the difference between the "inside dream" of personal visions and feelings with the "outside dream" of the conventions of society. Reason is the software program that seeks to harmonize differences between your interior and exterior world. For example, let's say you have an "inside dream" to take a vacation, but the "outside dream" of colleagues pressure you to continue to work. What's to be done? Typically, reason steps in to make you harmonize with the outside world even at the cost of suppressing your own feelings. With the ever-changing complexities of life, reason strives to help you feel safe by declaring more boundaries, definitions, and evaluations to establish a modicum of order and control in an ever-accelerating world.

What is problematical is that even if the conventional wisdoms of society are delusional, reason will still go along to accommodate the "inside dream" of your psyche with the "outside dream" of society so that you can feel secure and function in the world. That is its job.

Society, however, *is* often delusional. For example, it wasn't too long ago that the world was assumed to be flat, that we were born in "original sin," and that women were considered second-class citizens. And, in our day, one persistent misconception is that only the material world is "real"—"Will you stop talking about dreams. I'm in the *real* world." In spite of whatever madness our society maintains, reason still strives to make us conform by creating rationale so that we can function in the world as it is.

This is why so many sages and seers see the ego as an obstacle to personal freedom, and urge us to "wake up" from the dysfunctional conventions of the world. By the time we reach maturity, however, we so believe in the ego's version of who we are that we're oblivious to how we've become imprisoned by its limitations. Feelings, *Being,* imagination and intuition, by now, are typically dismissed by the ego because they lie beyond the pale of intellect and can't be reasonably controlled.

> *"The greatest flaw of human beings is to remain glued to the inventory of reason. Reason doesn't deal with man as energy. Reason deals with instruments that create energy, but it has never seriously occurred to reason that we are better than instruments: we are organisms that create energy. We are bubbles of energy."*
>
> —don Juan, Castaneda

And yet, even with all its traps, the formation of an ego is an essential first step if we are to function in the world. *A healthy ego must first be developed before it can be transcended.*

> *Behold the gifts of ego:*
> *Discernment—so innocence may navigate the world;*
> *Forbearance—so sensitivity may endure the setbacks of life;*
> *Individuality—so eternity may remember the rich riot of time.*

To be clear, reason and ego in themselves are not to be disparaged. They are essential to balance budgets, keep appointments and function in the practical necessities of daily life. Furthermore, the creation of masterworks in art, architecture, and science would not be possible without it. The problem arises only when it takes over our life like a tyrant by denying emotions, Spirit, and dreams. When we can make it act properly in *service* to the heart, then it becomes a powerful and essential ally.

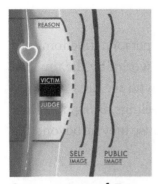

Components of Ego
Checkpoints and "allies" to maintain control.

In Map 5, the yellow part of the mind, *Reason,* faces outward towards the *Exterior World* to acknowledge its role of helping us function in the outside world. The purple area of *Intuition* faces the *Interior World*.

In view of the complex challenges of life, reason requires a methodology and "assistants" to fulfill its function. It set up a number of checkpoints and "allies" to help it maintain control. Four of the most prominent are the *Judge*, the *Victim*, and the *Self* and *Public Image*. All together, they comprise the main components of the ego.

In Map 5, within the yellow-orange area of the ego lie the key elements that form the ego: the *Judge* and *Victim* are seen as a red and black square, respectively, and the *Self* and *Public Image*, are each shown as a green, wavy line. They are wavy because they distort the arrows of desire. Exiled to the outside of this yellow-orange territory lie the *Emotional Body, Intuition,* and the *Heart*.

The Judge and Victim

Contemporary life confronts us with so much to evaluate, and so little time to decide. To assess what is life-enhancing from what is life-debilitating, and what is true from what is false, reason set up a "Judge" with the authority to make discernments on all aspects of life including appointments, vocation, opinions, values, and people.

However, due to the overwhelming influence of parental upbringing, media and religion, our power to assess differences between *truth and illusion* quickly became perverted to judgments between *good and evil*. Discernment turned into judgment. Instead of saying, "I don't like that movie," we end up declaring, "That movie is a ridiculous failure!." The cumulative effect of this tendency to pass judgment can be seen in the public arena where scandal magazines are a multi-billion dollar business, the blog-o-sphere is rife with accusations, lawyers demand increasingly exorbitant fees, and everything is open to judgment, including loved ones, celebrities, the entire Middle East, the sun, and God.

This propensity to judge does not *have* to happen. In the case of Alicia discussed earlier, when she first took a driving test, she failed! It was a crushing blow for her because she was so used to excelling in all she did. She started beating herself up—her Judge had seized the moment—until her father suggested to her that this may be as important a lesson as any she had learned in school: How to *fail nobly*. Everybody "fails" at one time or another, but failure doesn't really exist if you don't give up. Suddenly, she gained a bigger perspective and could laugh it off. Any inclination for Alicia's Judge to wrack havoc with her was nipped in the bud.

As a natural complement to the Judge (who generally finds everyone guilty), ego has also set up the "Victim" whose original, pristine role was to be able to endure all the betrayals, setbacks, and tragedies that flesh is heir to, i.e. *forbearance* (the ability to withstand adversity). However, thanks to the Judge, what was originally forbearance turned into victimhood—"No one understand me…Life is so unfair…I'm such an outsider, a freak … Screwed up again…" As we shall soon see, the ego for most people will become increasingly tyrannical. With its two "appointees" of the Judge and the Victim, it will set up the key causes of the vast majority of our malaise.

In Map 5, **Formation of Ego**, these "allies" of reason, the *Judge* and the *Victim*, are shown in the two squares colored blood red and black, respectively. They are square in shape to denote the hard–edged primal nature of judgment and guilt.

> *As all tyrants were once benign*
> *So, too, ego comes to love power.*
> *Its allies, Victim and the Judge,*
>   *can deny all else their rightful hour.*

Public Image

Through parents, schooling and media from an early age, we learned to cultivate a public image. As infants, we imitated our parents, and strived to look like little grown-ups. As we matured, we kept adjusting our persona to fit in with peers, potential lovers, and authorities. What must we do to look well in the eyes of the world? Change clothes? Lovers? Cars? Neighborhoods?

Many spend their whole lives trying to keep up with some illusory, external idea of how they should appear in the world. Media advertisements goad us persistently to "improve" our public image. Learning fast, we adapted accordingly, and more or less moved in step with our peers. We felt successful, we belonged and gained confidence in how we appeared to the world…at least for a while.

Ultimately, belief in our public image will prove unfulfilling because it is still an image. A costume. Not the essence of who we are. Still, we need a persona to function in the world. The attitude on how to maintain a public image without undermining the truth of who we are can be expressed by the Biblical aphorism, "be *in* the world but not *of* the world." Create your persona, as you must, but don't believe for a second that it's the real you.

Self-image

Similar to our Public Image, we are always shifting our Self Image. It had begun since early childhood when we were impressionable and swallowed wholesale judgments, condemnation and humiliation by parents, teachers, and peers. In dark moments of solitude, we still nurse those secret wounds that the world had aroused—unworthiness, guilt, poverty, shame. And, contrarily, secret dreams, visions and noble aspirations. All these private feelings are kept secret because revealing them would make us feel way too vulnerable. Thanks to the ego, however, we have somewhere to file them away, *Self Im-*

age. For our eyes only. Even though peace comes when the inner and outer image agree, for most people they are tragically at odds.

In Map 5, we see between the Interior and Exterior World two wavy green lines—*Self Image* and *Public Image.* They are shown wavy because they distort all our perceptions and desires. If, for example, someone secretly felt insecure and weak, his arrows of desire would become distorted going through the line of Self Image. To express such patterns of distortion, notice in the map how the arrows labeled *Impulse of Desire,* and *Reaction to Outcome* are also shown bent off course as they go through the *Self* and *Public Image.*

How the ego comes to power
As children, our natural tendency is to live in the eternal present. But, as described above, that innocence gradually diminishes as we begin to cultivate the intellect and the ego. Typically, this development begins when we are given a name, which helps to distinguish us as a separate individual apart from the rest of society—In the whole, wide world, we are each one-of-a-kind! With that name comes the seed of the ego, self–identity, and separation. (For some, the seeds of ego began even before birth when personal names were already decided upon.)

This fundamental illusion of separation—the root cause of so much later suffering—continued when we learned to categorize and make definitions on our own behalf beginning with "*I* am, *I* want, *I* will, and *my* name, *my* house, *my* parents." In this spirit, we continued our journey to develop a personal will and ego, all essential if we are to find our place in the world. Attuned to the values championed by society, we try to stand out, be a rebel, be distinguished, be number one.

By the time we become reasonably successful, we have assumed that we *are* our ego. We take for granted that our ego will continue to lead us upward and onward to fulfill our dreams. Furthermore, secretly driven by hidden pains and sorrows, we entrust ego to somehow help us find relief from our private sorrows by becoming more outwardly successful. After all, isn't this what the whole world does?

> *O, how the heart smolders*
> *With boundless private pain.*
> *If only success would end all torment—*
>   *such hopes we harbor in ego's domain.*

Giving ego newfound responsibilities, we allow it to expand its control over our entire life. With our blessing, it moves through the world pretending to be us. When it declares that our fulfillment depends on a new car or career, we go along trusting it is speaking for our best interest and automatically obey its dictates.

In Map 5, the dominance of the yellow-orange territory of the *Ego* represents the situation described above when one's entire life begins to fall under its spell. *Reason, Self* and *Public Image, Judge* and *Victim,* by now, are shown all working together to fulfill one's ambition in the world according to ego.

The despotic ego
Unbeknownst to us, however, this increasing identity with ego's version of success and failure opens us to feeling unappreciated, lonely, and judged, a natural outcome of someone driven to being distinctive and separate. We begin to hear our Judge berating us for not measuring up to ego's idealized version of ourself: "Why aren't you more rich and famous by now? Why are you so fat? So clumsy?"

Regardless of the tyrannical voice of the ego, we notice that our "successes" are so unfulfilling and temporary, and our disappointments so painful (especially with that Judge condemning us further for our failures) that after a few years we have to admit that in spite of all our precious accomplishments and possessions, we cannot fill a growing emptiness inside. Deep down, we begin to feel disillusioned, lost, and miserable.

But our ego, a full-blown tyrant by now, makes us struggle on, "Don't be a wimp. Look at that celebrity. He made it, you can, too!" If we try to rebel against ego's (and society's) idea of success, punishments and rewards force us to reassess and toe the line. If we lost our job, for instance, instead of feeling our loss, we would worry more over what others may think and the unbearable shame we must endure. Looking around, however, we see everyone racing ahead wasting no time indulging in "navel-gazing," and so we, too, plunge back into the fray ever more determined to seize our portion of wealth and fame in spite of our misgivings.

Through the years as we become increasingly identified with the ego's idea of who we are, we have completely forgotten our source in Being. The ego has taken over our psyche, tells us what we can and cannot do, and what we are allowed to think. Dreams, intuition, emotions, love, stillness and joy all open us to our source in Being and the magnanimity of who we are, but since they extend beyond the reach of *reason*, they are routinely dismissed by the ego because…they are so "unreasonable."

The ego also considers only that part of the psyche that is *conscious*, and routinely denies what is subconscious or transcendent. If we have a vision, for example, the ego challenges it by declaring, "It's only a dream," or, "Prove it." For the ego, master–minded by reason, everything has to be logical, practical, and quantifiable. We have fallen under the spell of what Deepak Chopra calls the "tyranny of reason."

In Map 5, *Intuition, Heart* and our Source in *Being* are shown largely ignored and banished outside the yellow-orange area of the ego. The line of the *Emotional Body* is at the edge of the *Ego,* serving as its borderline. This reflects how the thinking mind *does* interact with emotions, but only tangentially, and often only to restrain the free flow of feelings, or to justify its right to exist.

The consequence of this limited self–identity is suffering. That is why sages and seers the world over have repeatedly suggested an understanding of what the ego is, and what it is not, and urged liberation from its hold over us.

To truly "know thyself," is a momentous task. Although wisdom traditions constantly warn against the traps of the ego, still, at the beginning we had to spend years cultivating it before we could move beyond it for our liberation. We can't skip a step, we can't transcend the ego unless we have one that functions well enough to transcend.

For most people, the *primary purpose* in life—to realize our true nature—has long been upstaged and repressed by our ego. By now, it is totally immersed in the *secondary purposes* of our life such as career moves, personal projects, and demands of the family.

In time, we will learn to prioritize our values by reinstating our heart on the throne, and have reason and ego be its loyal and powerful servant. This liberation from ego's over-reach will be taken up in the next few chapters. For now, to show how we got here, we'll trace the pathway of the *Formation of Ego*. How does our psyche react when, for example, we have a desire, but it's thwarted?

> The coup complete, ego claims the regal seat,
> Where are the Guardians to redress this wrong?
> What brave deeds can fulfill our silent knowing?
> On that throne the wounded Heart belongs.

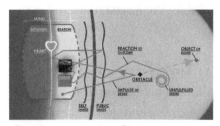

The "Bounce-Back"
The complexity of psychological reactions.

In Map 5, a red arrow is propelled from the yellow area of *Reason* towards its *Object of Desire*. Imagine a student, envious of his classmates, who thinks that he, too, deserves to have a girlfriend. Attracted to a young lady, he musters the courage to ask her out…

With the aid of the blueprint, we can peek into the secret workings of his mind by following his *Impulse of Desire*. Since the student's motivation was predominantly an *idea* rather than a feeling, it launches from the area of *Reason*.

"Excuse me, but are you free Friday? I would love to get to know you, maybe over a cup of coffee?"

"Well…" she ponders as she checks him out, "I don't know…"

After a moment's hesitation, he lets out his breath, and coolly runs his fingers through his hair. Like a computer, he had already made a dozen calculations in his mind even before she had finished her sentence. It all happened at the speed of light. Slowing down the exchange, however, we can see it as a typical pattern that so many of us go through all the time with a thousand variations. This complex interplay between all components of the ego and the emotional, mental and physical bodies—the "Bounce-Back"—is something we do unconsciously day in and day out.

In Map 5, the red arrow shoots out towards his Object of Desire (getting a date), but immediately experiences an "obstacle" due to her hesitation. The arrow doubles back to the man's…

> *Emotional Body* (the man feels sad and disappointed), then bounces through…
> *Reason* ("You miscalculated. She just isn't into you."), as the…
> *Physical Body* (slumps, stomach growls); the arrows continues to his…
> *Public Image* (he feigns nonchalance), and falls prey to…
> *Victim* ("I'm just a Geek and Geeks never get the girl."), back to his…
> *Reason* ("You're wasting time from your studies."), to bounce off the…
> *Judge* ("All your smarts and you can't even get a girl,") to…
> *Self-Image* ("Face it, I'm too fat, square and poor for romance"), and on to…
> *Public Image* (acts cool, runs fingers through his hair), as finally, the…
> *Impulse of Desire* spirals into nothing, (he's kissed her off).

All this happens at breakneck speed, a process that can be utterly stressful, and done repeatedly during a single hour. But then, the woman finishes her sentence,

"But I'd love to on Saturday. On Friday, I have to take care of my Dad." Our hero lights up! A completely new set of reactions is triggered with "Bounce-Back" reactions among all the components of the ego. He stands taller, feels confident, worthy…

This incident is only one exchange. During the course of a single day, there are dozens more with parents, teachers, classmates, and a boss, each with their own dynamics, often overlapping, many contradictory. This is how the ego whips us on through life with the unending illusion that to be happy, we need something from the exterior world. Filled with judgment, stress, and frustration, it's a wonder anything gets done.

Still, driven by insatiable longings, we push on seeking relief by grasping for more. The next map will show the outcome of such unrelenting desires.

* * *

6. TYRANNY OF DESIRE

I count him braver who overcomes his desires
than him who conquers his enemies,
for the hardest victory is over self.

—Aristotle

This chapter addresses the inner condition of most of us. We want so much, and yet many of our desires are impulsive, self-defeating and contradictory. Fanned by society and media, our default position is to resolve our misgivings by wanting and acquiring more. "I'd be happy if only I had the latest smart phone, a faster car, a larger house,..." Cumulatively, as a society, it's a situation that threatens our very survival.

But what's wrong with longing for world peace, a happy family, or self-realization? Nothing whatsoever, which brings up a good question: What *do* we want? Is it for something bigger than ourselves, or for self-importance? Is it for our heart or our ego?

"Without desire, movement is not possible.
Even wishing for happy life, a happy life for others –
all is desire. Desire leads our action."

—Dalai Lama

It is not desire, per se, that causes suffering, but the nature of our longings that is the problem. Most of us already sense the traps of desire (at least intellectually), and yet, for various reasons, we're still driven to carry on and accumulate things. Whatever the cause (we'll soon look into this deeply), the consequence of this insatiable consumption has sabotaged our happiness personally as well as our survival globally.

As with all maps that help us when we're lost by stating *You are here*, we hereby present with unblinking candor Map 6, *Tyranny of Desire...*

LEGEND · PART TWO : LOST & CONFUSED

Map 6: TYRANNY OF DESIRES

In *Tyranny of Desire*, a flood of red arrows representing a wide spectrum of yearnings pours forth in every direction. Their trajectories distort as they pass through the *Judge, Victim, Self* and *Public Image* and create a confusing array of overlapping and contradictory pathways. Those unfulfilled end as spirals.

The *Ego, Judge* and *Victim* have all deepened in color to signify their growing dominance. The vast majority of desires and distortions occur within the *Ego's* territory of control, as represented by the orange oval.

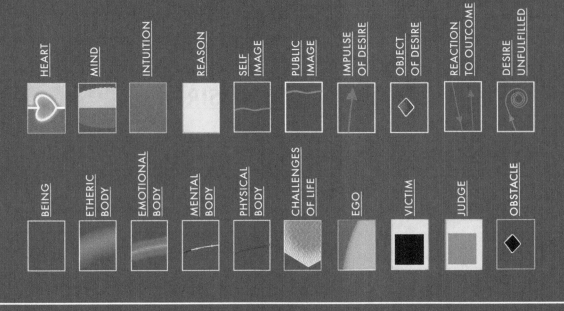

BEING	HEART	
ETHERIC BODY	MIND	
EMOTIONAL BODY	INTUITION	
MENTAL BODY	REASON	
PHYSICAL BODY	SELF IMAGE	
CHALLENGES OF LIFE	PUBLIC IMAGE	
EGO	IMPULSE OF DESIRE	
VICTIM	OBJECT OF DESIRE	
JUDGE	REACTION TO OUTCOME	
OBSTACLE	DESIRE UNFULFILLED	

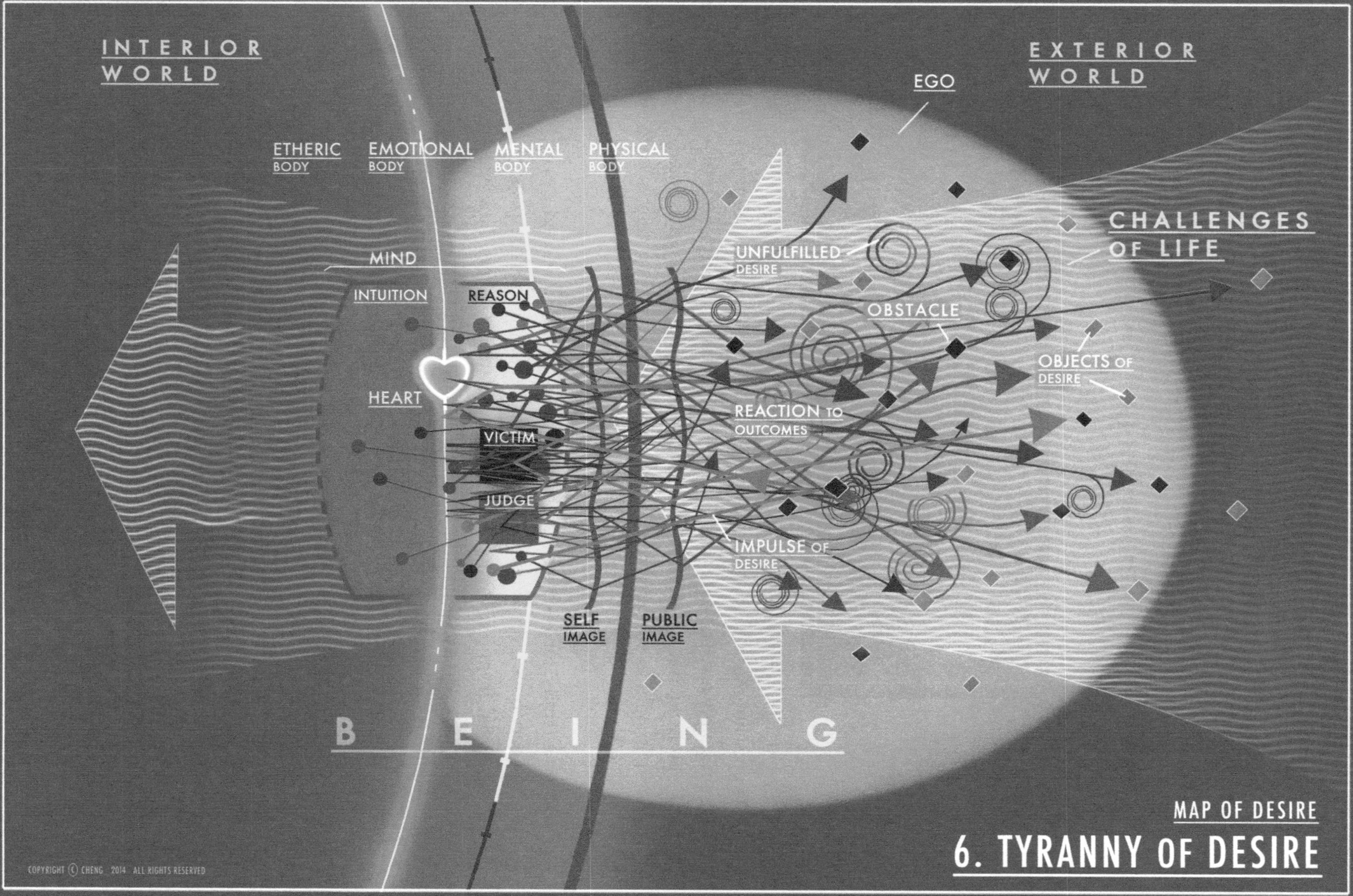

INTERIOR WORLD

EXTERIOR WORLD

CHALLENGES OF LIFE

EGO

OBJECTS OF DESIRE

OBSTACLE

UNFULFILLED DESIRE

REACTION TO OUTCOMES

IMPULSE OF DESIRE

PUBLIC IMAGE

SELF IMAGE

PHYSICAL BODY

ETHERIC BODY

EMOTIONAL BODY

MENTAL BODY

MIND

REASON

INTUITION

VICTIM

JUDGE

HEART

BEING

MAP OF DESIRE

6. TYRANNY OF DESIRE

A flood of desires

The thicket of arrows represents all our desires. It's a situation that has gone amuck. How much hard work, heartaches, disappointments and waste it represents! And how tragic that for all the time and money we spend on worldly ambition and outer pursuits, all the most important things we want—love, peace, wisdom, beauty—are qualities that can only be found within.

> *Romance, wealth, respect, and fame*
> *How we hunger for all our dreams require.*
> *Yet, to seek fulfillment from beyond ourselves*
> *   is delusion that leads to the tyranny of desire.*

This does not mean that careers, families, and projects are not significant, because they most certainly are. They are where we spend the vast majority of our time and resources, and rightly so, but ultimately, their true value can only be determined by what fulfillment it brought to our *primary objectives*: How much did they help us awaken to who we really are?

Raising a family, for instance, can help us not only in our secondary objectives, but also our primary ones if the experience opens our heart towards compassion. We would then feel liberated from our own ego needs as we care for others. However, that same family involvement may mean little if it's only an act of blind obedience to parents or social conventions, or to create appearances of stability and responsibility with no joy or love involved.

But ego, media, and social pressure pay scant attention to "primary objectives," and convince you that you'll find happiness if you'd only buy this device or that product. In dreaming of love, for example, you may find yourself driven to purchase a late-model convertible to go with your stylish clothes and platinum watch, all to be complemented by a nice apartment with a fashionable zip code so as to impress the fantasy lover of your dreams. All this requires money, of course, which instigates a new flood of desires involving power-lunches with people that count so that your career will impress and, in spite of anxieties within, you'll be able to walk and talk like a great man of success convinced that by so doing you can attract "the one" who can fulfill the yearning for love you so longed for in the first place.

Or, you could simply love yourself the way you are.

To accept and love ourselves, free of self-judgment even as we change and grow—this is a secret dream we all carry within, if we could only put it in practice. It is a goal that can completely change our lives.

> *Still something stirs*
> *A breath of fresh air*
> *Yes, fortune favors those who seek,*
>   *and glorifies those who dare.*

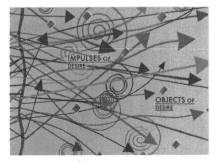

Tyranny of Desire
Insatiable hunger for more.

In Map 6, the flood of arrows shooting out in every direction represents this plethora of wants. Representing how so many of our desires are at cross-purposes with each other, the arrows cross and contradict each other.

"Dream of the planet"

If it is so apparent that gross consumerism won't make us happy, why are so many of us under its spell? Because for every cry from that small inner voice of another way to live, there are a thousand opposing ones from the media and the multi-billion dollar marketing industry. Belief in materialism along with the fear, greed and delusions that drives us towards mindless consumption is a characteristic of what Toltec shamans call the "dream of the planet." This phrase expresses the cumulative "dreams" of millions of individuals, that combine at first to create "family dreams"—the assumptions, habits, and beliefs of that family—which in turn combine into a "dream of the community," and then of the nation, and ultimately of the entire planet.

In our day, this "dream of the planet" is more like a nightmare filled with insatiably materialistic people who continually struggle to win at any cost, and consume with no restraint. Ethics are barely considered in the face of this gross consumerism, so corruption and greed are a natural consequence. Multiplied a million times, it is not surprising that our world is undergoing the tremendous problems of our times—the financial debacle, global warming, and growing disparity of the "haves and have-nots."

The Buddha saw this syndrome ages ago when he proclaimed as his *Second Noble Truth* (the first being that "suffering exists") that the cause of suffering is *trishna*, the constant grasping for something outside of ourselves because we think we are incomplete.

A classic example of this in our times is our current worship of celebrities and "Super Stars." If we are to believe the media, they have it all, they're "rich and famous," and their every gesture studied and imitated. Some of us may feel affronted by their antics, and scoff at the hype, but part of their message has already slipped in, subliminally, that fulfillment depends on some form of acquisition from outside of us.

Although time and again, it has been revealed that all is not well in the paradise of our Super Stars—violence, drugs, anxiety, and depression often fill their lives—their image of success inspires millions to strive for what they have, and buy what they endorse. Those Super Stars who are truly fulfilled due to inner values *in spite* of their stardom, the media generally ignores. They are not deemed newsworthy.

In Map 6 of this chapter, the darkening of the color of the *Ego* from the yellow of the preceding map to the deep orange here reflects the increased and heavier burden the ego imposes on the individual. Because the ego believes all solutions to emotional/psychological needs can best be found in the materialistic world of form, it provokes the plethora of red arrows.

A contrary opinion
Yet, deep within, we have a tiny voice crying out courageously that what truly matters—love, beauty, peace, fulfillment—can only come from the heart within. This desperate plea to consider our "primary cause" has been heard many times before, but our increasingly tyrannical ego can't be bothered, "Stop whining. Cut that spiritual mumble-jumble. Time is money!" If such a voice dares to speak out in society, then the "ego" of society will often strike it down, as Lincoln, Gandhi, and Christ experienced.

> *Enter the hero, dressed as the Fool*
> *Ever ridiculed, undermined, and deceived*
> *Awakens the wrath of the world,*
>   *society being ruled by a consensus of the aggrieved.*

Driven by the ego, bewitched by consumerism, we become workaholics and alcoholics to try and fill our emptiness with material goods. We spend money we don't have to buy things we don't need until forced to rent storage to keep all we don't want. Is this not a sign of madness?

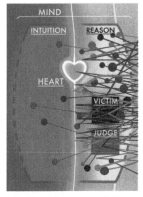

Components of Ego
Checkpoints and "allies" to maintain control

In Map 6, the flood of red arrows of desires (often intertwined with thoughts, accusations, defenses, and mind chatter) shoot forth from within the yellow area of Reason. Very few launch from the *Heart* or the purple area of *Intuition* for the ego has taken over and is intent on fulfilling its own agenda.

Looking within

In spite of the obsessed drive for outer success, that small brave voice continues to cry out on behalf of hidden heart needs that seek loving care rather than more objects. After years of neglect, it is no wonder that many people are susceptible to sudden outbursts of pain, rage, envy, or bouts of anxiety and despair. If heart wounds are still left untended, physical ailments begin to appear—worries produce ulcers and stresses cause heart attacks.

For those of us who are finally able to look *within* to address our torments, a whole new world opens up. We often see that all our striving for outer success was driven by basic inner longings—the need to be acknowledged, to have meaning in our lives, or to be loved. Many of these yearnings have been repressed for years because we have been too busy trying to fulfill our longings through outer consumption and careers. This long, painful shadow cast over entire adult lives have become so familiar that for many, it is much easier to endure a familiar pain than to break out into unknown territory for true happiness. In Men's Conferences prevalent in the nineties, for example, time and again men revealed how they had devoted decades of their life striving for success in order to prove, unbeknownst to themselves, that they were worthy in the eyes of a critical, abusive, or missing parent.

From a shamanic point of view, these untended wounds are seen as parasites, or *inner demons* sabotaging us from within. Carl Jung called them the *shadow* since these unresolved wounds can remain hidden in our blind spots for years. Typically, these wounds distort our self and/or public image, ("I'm unworthy," or *"I'm* the one in control"), or fill us with self–judgment and/or victimhood ("When am I ever going to get it together?" "What a wimp I am!" or "Why am I always the fall guy?"). Sooner or later, the truth hits us directly: Our worst enemies are the inner demons within.

> *So be forewarned,*
> *The battles now set to begin*
> *What brutality suffered from others*
> *   a pale reflection of our saboteurs within.*

A tremendous amount of personal power is spent dealing with these hidden saboteurs either by trying to alleviate the pains they've caused, protect them from being touched, or deny their existence. How much simpler it is, typically, to blame someone else for our disappointments rather than take responsibility and face our own demons. As a consequence, we find fault with the world rather than look within.

> *"Self-importance is man's greatest enemy. What weakens him*
> *is feeling offended by the deeds and misdeeds of his fellow men.*
> *Self-importance requires that one spend most of one's life*
> *offended by something or someone."*
>
> —don Juan, Castaneda

In this Map 6, *Tyranny of Desire*, the torment from all those inner demons can be seen in the dizzy array of red arrows with all their "Bounce-Back" between the *Self* and *Public Image, Judge, Victim, Reason* and the *Emotional Body*. As seen in the preceding Map 5, *Formation of Ego*, even one conversation (not to mention arguments) can produce a complex reaction between all components of the ego, and for most of us, we undergo dozens of interactions each day, some with repercussions that may go on for years. Altogether, they produce the accumulation of red arrows we see in the map.

What's to be done?
Our ego's reaction to inner pain is to avoid addressing it directly and blame something outside of ourselves for our misery. Ego's existence thrives on such conflict and so, denying our personal distress, our ego forces us to soldier on in the competitive marketplace. Finally, however, after we are truly sick of suffering, after we are forced to admit that we are lost and confused, we commit to the "quest" with high hopes.

However, after only a few steps on this quest, we are inundated with a barrage of contradictory advice—should we "Take action and make it happen," or "Let go and let God?" Is it true that "money is the root of all evil?" or is "money a part of nature's abundance and our birthright?" How do we make informed decisions? How can we gain clarity between our "primary" and "secondary" objectives?

> *How, then, will the treaties be made?*
> *How will the peace ever come?*
> *In defeat and despair*
> *grow the seeds of wisdom.*

In moments like these, what we truly need are time-tested roadmaps so that we can make our own informed decisions. The next several maps show three clear pathways distilled from wisdom traditions East and West. They have proven effective for millennia, and can lead us from confusion and fear into personal freedom.

* * *

PART THREE
FINDING OUR WAY OUT

Up to now, we've explored *Where are we?* and *How did we get here?* Given the upheaval we find in our world, we admit to feeling lost and confused, which gives rise to a new yearning: *What's the way out?*

Distilled from the wisdom of the ages, the next several maps depict three clear pathways to personal freedom that have proven effective through years of workshops. They'll help you break through the uncertainty of our times and lead you towards inner peace and Self-Fulfillment.

7. ATTUNEMENT TO BEING

At the center of your being you have the answer;
You know who you are and you know what you want.

—Lao Tzu

What is Attunement to Being?
This phrase means to be in harmony with Spirit, or our Source in Being. By getting back in touch with our Source, we can consciously access the infinite energy, intelligence, and love of the universe to flow through us to vitalize our lives much more powerfully.

Imagine a tree sick with brown leaves. Many deny that there's a problem, others suggest cutting off branches with the worst leaves, while some even argue to paint the leaves green for an immediate solution. All their suggestions, regardless of their merits, consider only the visible symptoms of the problem. This is the way of most of society, beholden as it is to the physical world of appearance as the ultimate reality.

Attunement to Being, however, seeks to address problems at their root causes in the invisible realm rather than on the surface level of their symptoms. Just like the tree's plight can be solved only by watering and fertilizing its unseen roots, our problems can be resolved only by connecting to our unseen roots in Being. Invisible and abstract as it may seem, it holds the key to our healing, harmony, and happiness.

Though over the years we might have built up in our psyche layers upon layers of ego desires, old wounds, and delusional thinking, by attuning to Being we can cut cleanly through our thicket of confusion because it engages us on a much deeper level of consciousness. To see this graphically, we have here Map 7, *Attunement to Being...*

LEGEND · PART THREE : THE WAY OUT

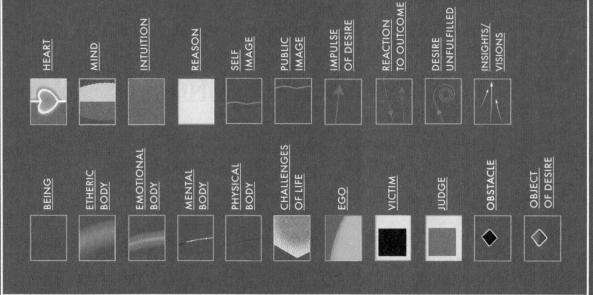

BEING · ETHERIC BODY · EMOTIONAL BODY · MENTAL BODY · PHYSICAL BODY · CHALLENGES OF LIFE · EGO · VICTIM · JUDGE · OBSTACLE · OBJECT OF DESIRE

HEART · MIND · INTUITION · REASON · SELF IMAGE · PUBLIC IMAGE · IMPULSE OF DESIRE · REACTION TO OUTCOME · DESIRE UNFULFILLED · INSIGHTS/VISIONS

Map 7: ATTUNEMENT TO BEING

This map expresses the first of three pathways towards personal freedom. From the *Heart* (situated just outside the area of *Ego*), a white arrow labeled *Desire from Being* launches forth. Its trajectory distorts as it moves through the *Self* and *Public Image*, but cuts cleanly through the orange territory of *Ego* towards its *Object of Desire* (colored white).

However, its path is repelled by the *Obstacle* (colored black). The trajectory of its return, marked *Reaction to Outcome*, enters into the purple area of *Intuition* where the three small arrows denote insights and visions from the universe. The "Bounce-Back" between elements of the ego is greatly simplified compared to the preceding map.

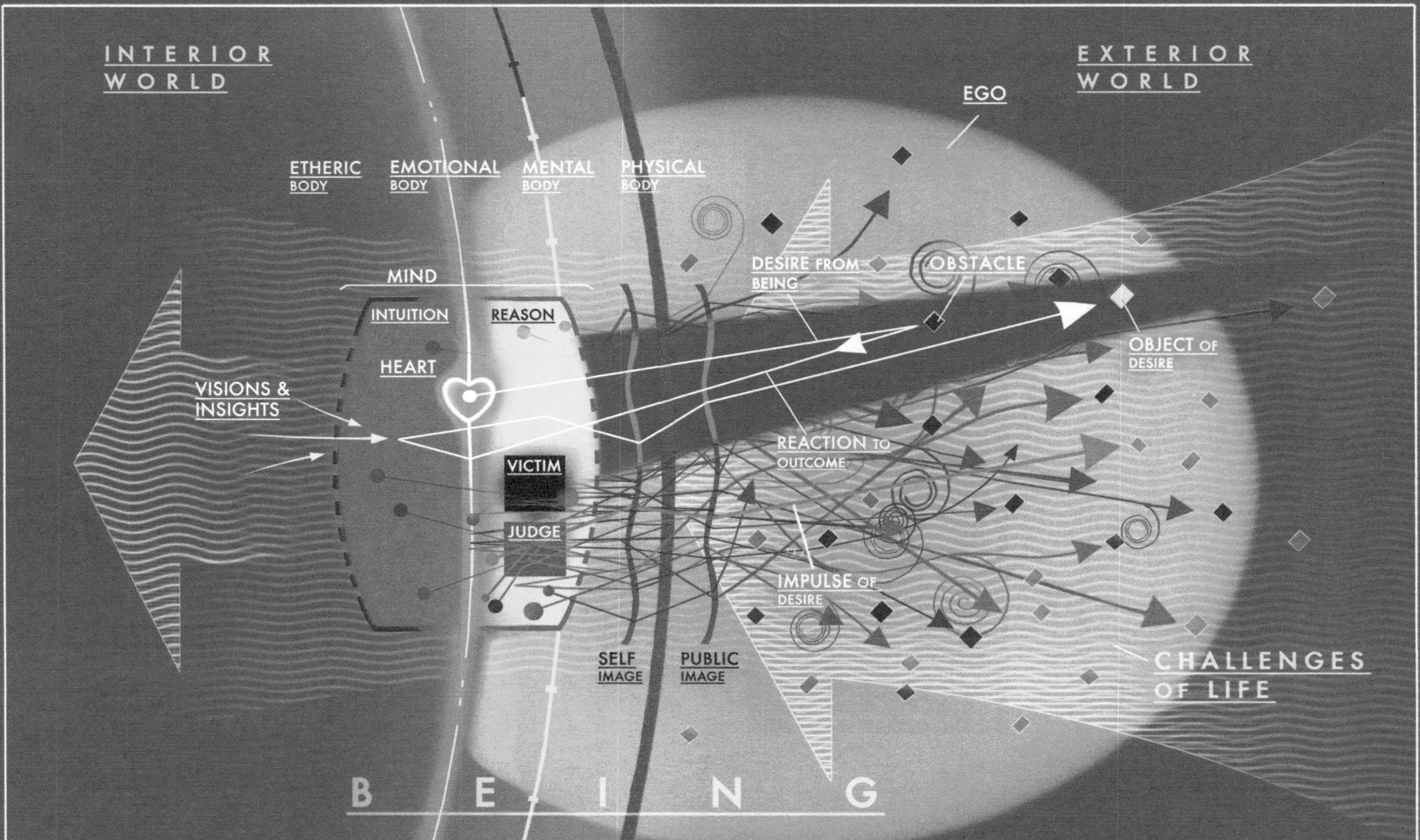

INTERIOR WORLD

EXTERIOR WORLD

EGO

OBSTACLE

OBJECT OF DESIRE

DESIRE FROM BEING

REACTION TO outcome

IMPULSE OF DESIRE

CHALLENGES OF LIFE

PHYSICAL BODY

ETHERIC BODY

MENTAL BODY

EMOTIONAL BODY

MIND

INTUITION

HEART

REASON

VICTIM

JUDGE

SELF IMAGE

PUBLIC IMAGE

VISIONS & INSIGHTS

B E I N G

7. ATTUNEMENT TO BEING

MAP OF DESIRE

Benefits from attuning to Being

One of the first benefits of connecting to Being is the liberation of your heart, intuition, feelings, and imagination. With these modes of perception, you again have the means to know your *feelings* about things (and not just their facts), and to gain direct access to the vastness and intelligence of the universe through heart and intuition. Insights and visions, then, come to you spontaneously, which can redirect your whole life, solve problems, spark masterworks, and/or reveal your true purpose on earth. Because of the nature of intuition and imagination, these insights come effortlessly while greatly expanding your reach into the universe.

> *Attunement to Being*
> *Shifts our gaze to the Source, an echo of the soul.*
> *We sense ourselves anew, then*
> *   from the viewpoint of the whole.*

Another benefit from attuning to Being is compassion. Once you attune to Being, you can blast through the ego's tendency to keep you separated from everyone else. Like a detached witness, you'll see a greatly expanded version of yourself intertwined with everyone else and the whole planet. Perhaps you suddenly realize a simple but powerful truth about your connection to your fellow human beings: We're all alike; *we suffer the same*. And *aspire* the same: Do we not all want acknowledgement, love, security, and meaningful work in our life? Instead of separation that your ego insists upon, you see that your well-being is directly connected with the well-being of your community. Once such patterns are perceived, compassion flows naturally towards everyone. With compassion, you gain a solid basis for any true contribution you want to make for society.

A third benefit from *Attunement to Being* is that Spirit becomes a co-creator in all your endeavors. With personal will aligned with that of Spirit, the infinite creative powers of the universe begin to flow through you. By allowing your intuition and imagination to tap into the supreme "organizing principle" of the universe, synchronicity and "lucky accidents" begin to be a way of life. A book falls in your lap, or you meet someone by chance, and the course of your life changes. All the qualities of the universe—integrity, harmony, radiance—become increasingly a part of you.

> *Intuition re-awakened,*
> *Inspiration trued by bold decree*
> *We stalk the universe for any clue*
> *that might reveal a sacred destiny.*

With the new perspective that *Attunement to Being* brings, you receive an unexpected bonus: your desires diminish. Yes indeed, there are many beautiful things in the world that you don't have to own. What you might have thought so essential and enduring has revealed itself to be but a passing fancy of little value.

On the other hand, these same "outer" achievements can provide lasting benefit, but only if they somehow help you fulfill "primary" goals such as giving you more heart or wisdom, perseverance or faith. Such values lie beyond the self-importance of the ego, and let you know *who you are* by revealing your higher angels.

> *"Everything looks permanent*
> *until its secret is known."*
>
> –Emerson

So, step-by-step, "five steps forward, two steps back," you free ourselves from the tyranny of reason, trust the wisdom of the heart, or your intuition—these two terms can be seen as synonymous—and attune to Being.

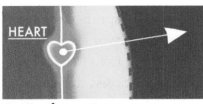

<u>Desire from Heart</u>
Fulfillment from beyond the ego.

In Map 7, *Attunement to Being*, freedom from ego desires can be seen with the white arrow launched from the *Heart*. The arrow is colored white, the hue used in mystical traditions to denote truth and purity. Shooting straight towards its *Object of Desire*, it cuts cleanly through the thicket of existing ego desires. Even when its trajectory is repelled by the obstacle, its Reaction to Outcome remains simple and direct.

Desires attuned to Being

In normal life, how can *Attunement to Being* cut through that thicket of ego desires as the map shows? It might appear simplistic, but it most certainly is not. By connecting with Being, forces much more subtle and powerful than ego—feelings, dreams, visions— come into play. Since ego is only *reason's* idea of who we are, our self-identity now becomes liberated beyond the limits of intellect and logic.

A classic example is seen in Martin Luther King's desire for racial equality. He was human; he wasn't blind to the ugly threats on his life. However, his ego's fear of death was trumped by his heart's desire to help humankind. Though he had been beaten and jailed many times, his attunement to a higher calling gave him great courage. (Courage is *not* about the absence of fear; it's about moving forward in spite it.) Whatever doubts and forebodings he may have held paled in comparison to his noble purpose. His will was aligned with that of Spirit's allowing him to move steadfastly towards his goal in spite of great adversity.

When you attune to Being and seek desires that transcend selfishness, this does not mean that you need to strive for grand ideas of social justice or political freedom (another trap of the ego if approached incorrectly). Instead, the key is to commit to your tasks big or small attuned to Being with total presence, faith, and heart. It's not *what* you do, but *how* you do it that takes us beyond the ego. As Mother Teresa reminds us, "It is not the magnitude of our actions, but the amount of love that is put into them that matters."

If you want material abundance, for example, the ego's motivation might be to hoard money for self-aggrandizement, whereas the heart's intent is to increase generosity for the family and community. As you attune to Being, inner attitudes often shift radically even if outer activities change but little.

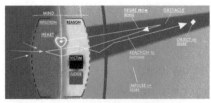

Desire from Beyond Ego
Attuning to powers of Being.

In Map 7, the white arrow shown here as launching from the heart could also have sprung from anywhere beyond the orange territory of the ego, such as the purple area of *Intuition,* or from the *Emotional Body,* both of which have direct access to *Being.* The three small arrows on the left denote powers from Being coming in to help the individual through insights and visions. Note that the *Emotional Body* is

94

situated closest to the *Interior World* to show that it is through looking within and accessing *feelings* that Spirit and Being can most directly be perceived.

Experiencing Being in daily life

Being is not only to be understood by the mind, but also to be *experienced*. This first requires an awareness that it exists. Like a cloud that obscures the radiance of the sun, our ego might have hidden Being from us for years or diminished its essence by confining it within the limits of reason, but still, like the sun, Being continues to radiate whether understood, acknowledged or dismissed.

To rediscover it, you must withdraw your attention from your ego long enough to allow heart, intuition, and imagination to reveal its perceptions. Then, like a cloud dissipating to reveal the sun, the illusion of ego will dissolve enough to reveal your everlasting connection to Being.

Complete step-by-step techniques to experience Being are offered under *Practices* towards the end of this book. For now as an overview, we will go over their basics:

Spend time in nature.

Nature is Being expressed in form. It's a living embodiment of integrity, harmony and beauty, so by opening yourself to nature you cannot help but absorb those qualities into your own psyche. To open to nature, remain silent. Stop talking and stop incessant mind chatter. Once silent, you can open your senses to the sounds, sights, and smells of plants and flowers all around. Everything has integrity. Everything is in harmony. Never has there been reported a tree that lies or complains about its upbringing. Your body knows and trusts its real mother, Mother Nature, and will naturally feel rejuvenated. From spending time in nature, all manner of inspiration and insights can spring up spontaneously.

Listen to your body

A second way to attune to Being is to listen to your body. By so doing, you bypass your thinking mind to receive direct physical responses you can feel. The body never lies. It is always communicating with you, if you listen. If truth is present, for instance, you might feel a shiver up the spine, or, goose bumps, or a lightness in the gait. If you're upset about something, your belly might growl, "I can't stomach that!" even if your mind tries to convince you that all is as it should be. Our bodies know.

Meditate

A third means to attune to Being is through meditation, a vast subject incorporating innumerable techniques and a variety of ends beyond the scope of this book. For our purposes, we need only note that meditation is a classic technique to turn your gaze inward, short-circuit the thinking mind, and reconnect you to your Source. In silence, Being is revealed.

Enter Sacred Space

A fourth technique to connect with Being is to enter "Sacred Space," a time-tested procedure to formally set aside your ego and daily concerns so you can make a direct connection with Spirit. Through altars, rituals, and/or invocations, there are as many ways to enter Sacred Space as there are people. In *Practices* at the end of this book, you will find complete, step-by-step instructions in all these techniques.

Who's on the throne?

One of the most practical ways to connect with Being, make decisions, and assess feelings during our daily life is to ask the question, *Who's on the throne?* Imagine, for example, that you're a sovereign, independent kingdom with a ruling body (reason, ego, intuition and heart) governing millions of your own subjects (cells, muscles and organs). In this vast complex of "subjects," each with their own desires and demands, the first question that arises is, "Who's in charge? Who's on the throne?"

Full of love and play as children of up to about three, your heart ruled the throne. Then, as mentioned before, to meet the challenges of life, parents, schooling, and society all taught you to develop your reason (and with it, the ego) in order to face those challenges. All unfolded as planned, except, one day a couple of decades later, you wake feeling empty inside. Perhaps your precious initial dreams for success in career and family had been met, but still you felt unfulfilled. How hard you worked towards your goals, so why did your accomplishments feel so hollow? What went wrong?

What could have happened was that through the years the ego had become so powerful that, unbeknownst to you, it had completely taken over the "kingdom" and usurped the throne. By the time you became an adult, your ego that had begun as an invaluable helpmate to your heart had turned into a self-obsessed tyrant. If, for example, you had a feeling about something—"I'm bored with this job,"—it might have been routinely dismissed and shoved to the background by your ego, "Keep working, you need the money." After a few years, you may have developed a growing rage at life for not ever having your feelings heard. Your heart had become suppressed by your ego.

When you attune to Being, you reinstate the heart back on the throne. With the heart comes all its allies including intuition, imagination, dreams and feelings. With reason and the ego repositioned to their proper function as servants to the heart, they can now be called upon by the heart as needed to fulfill practical demands in the material world (not to mention sublime aspirations in the creation of artistic projects). By so doing, your *un-evolved* ego (that tyrant on the throne) transforms into an *evolved* ego (a powerful servant to heart and Spirit).

This reinstating of your heart back on the throne also repositions your priorities of primary and secondary purposes of your life on earth. Once again, the quest for Self-realization—to *know thyself*—comes to the fore, which helps put in perspective all your other aspirations. (Again, see *Practices* at the end of this book for exercises that will allow you to experience Being.)

In Map 7, reinstating the heart as the power on the throne can be seen with the white arrow launched from the *Heart* rather than from the realm of the ego. The heart allows a direct connection to Being. The white arrow, *Reaction to Outcome,* also guided by the heart, bypasses the Judge, Victim, and other points in the realm of the ego and remains simple and direct.

Listening to the heart
How often we've been counseled to "listen to our heart." But this can sometimes appear simplistic because within the realm of the heart, there are many levels of feeling, pure and perverted, spontaneous and considered. For example, "Why should I listen to my heart if it is so filled with jealousy, envy or revenge?"

It is a great question. To answer, we want to first make a distinction between different levels of feelings. Those impulsive, knee-jerk emotions when someone cuts us off in traffic are *not* to be confused with profound stirrings in our heart that come from sublime music, natural beauty, or the presence of a beloved. One is spontaneous and involuntary, while the other involves an intelligence and assessment of value. Carl Jung refers to the first as *emotions* to distinguish it from the second, which he calls *feelings*. Just to know this distinction can be a great help in helping us avoid confusion about our own feelings.

With love, for example, the spontaneous, dizzy emotion when we "fall in love," can often be merely an idealized fantasy projection of the moment. Spontaneous and almost involuntary, this would be an example of *emotions* as defined above. Going by the vast majority of pop songs and films, many relations stop right here and go no deeper. This same experience of falling in love, however, may evolve into the deep, knowing love we experience that harbors no illusions and no conditions. This would be an example of *feelings* as noted above.

Returning to the question of jealousy, envy, and revenge, these feelings illustrate another complexity: they have become intertwined with *thoughts*. Delusional thoughts, for the most part. For instance, the feeling of love for a beloved if combined with the thought that "She's mine, she belongs to me..." will give rise to jealousy. Like a vine suffocating a healthy tree, such delusional thoughts can choke the feelings of a pure heart. To disentangle such thoughts from feeling can prove problematical. However, it is not necessary (and sometimes not possible) to disentangle such mental constructs from pure feelings; there are easier ways.

One classic process is to first attune to your Source in Being. This will give you perspective by reminding you to keep in mind the big picture. For example, if plagued by jealousy as mentioned above, you can first quiet the mind as you would do while meditating and attune to Spirit. This will make space for your psyche to unpack and reveal the jealousy with no judgment.

In this open space, you may suddenly experience fiery rage ("After all we've promised each other, how dare you! You've betrayed our trust!"). By simply being present with no judgment, self-pity, or "stories," your emotions will continue to evolve. After the anger blows out, perhaps you experience deep feelings of resentment or emotional pain, ("Didn't we have a thing going? I love you, but now I'm so hurt..."). Again, you would simply observe it with no judgment or self-pity, and watch it shift again.

Perhaps after awhile you receive flashes of insight that reveal new perspectives that lessen the weight of your problems. You may realize that *you* are the one causing the problem by imagining her unfaithfulness because of your insecurity and control issues, that she had been true to you all along. On the other hand, if she *did* have an affair, it's a wake-up call that something is lacking in your relationship, and that you should have a serious talk. (More on such personal matters in Chapter 9.)

In this Map 7, *Attunement to Being*, the simplicity of the trajectory of the white arrow shows that even though the ego loves complications, the truth from our heart is basically simple and powerful. The "Bounce-Back" pattern of *Reaction to Outcome* also remains minimal, and at one point enters into the purple area of *Intuition*, which further helps simplicity by providing direct solutions to our problems.

> *Attunement to Being defies logic and time*
> *Courting accident and effortless flow*
> *Genius conjured by mischief's wand,*
> *doing less, accomplishments grow.*

* * *

8. DETACHMENT FROM OUTCOMES

I exist as I am, that is enough,
If no other in the world be aware, I sit content,
And if each and all be aware, I sit content.

—Walt Whitman

Freedom from illusion

This chapter expresses the second of three clear paths to personal freedom. With detachment, we withdraw our attention from results to focus on the task at hand. By so doing, we save a tremendous amount of chi (personal power) that often becomes squandered on needless worry over what may or may not happen.

Detachment frees us from the "world of appearances," and the illusion of form. We pull back from the symptoms of our lives to focus on their root causes. It is in the emotional/ psychological realm where we'll find the joy, peace and love we crave because, after all, these qualities are all feelings. They come from within us or not at all.

With detachment, we also become free from expecting immediate returns for our labors. Life will no longer be lived as an investment in some imagined future (as our ego insists), but rather lived and enjoyed now, moment to moment.

In its obsession to maintain control, our ego remains blind to the simple fact that so much of what happens to us has nothing to do with us: Don't take things personally. When we begin to see through outcomes and appearances and accept what is, we begin to perceive the miracle of life in the most commonplace events. Here, then, is Map 8, *Detachment from Outcomes…*

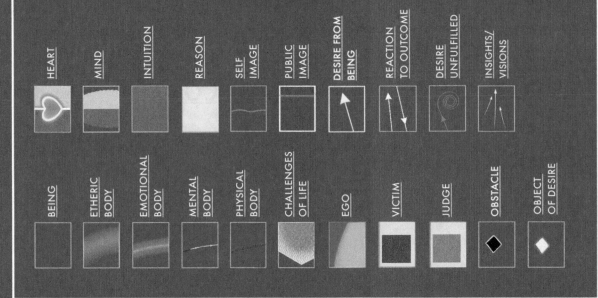

HEART

MIND

INTUITION

REASON

SELF IMAGE

PUBLIC IMAGE

DESIRE FROM BEING

REACTION TO OUTCOME

DESIRE UNFULFILLED

INSIGHTS/ VISIONS

BEING

ETHERIC BODY

EMOTIONAL BODY

MENTAL BODY

PHYSICAL BODY

CHALLENGES OF LIFE

EGO

VICTIM

JUDGE

OBSTACLE

OBJECT OF DESIRE

LEGEND · PART THREE : THE WAY OUT

Map 8: DETACHMENT FROM OUTCOMES

In Map 8, a white arrow emerges from the *Heart* and cuts cleanly through the yellow area of the *Ego*. As it passes through the green line labeled *Public Image* (now straight), the arrow shows no distortion on its way to its *Object of Desire*.

When its progress is thwarted by the *Obstacle*, its "Bounce-Back" among the elements of the *Ego* remains simple and direct. Its trajectory includes entry into the purple area of *Intuition* where one is open to *Visions* and *Insights*, as represented by the three small arrows coming in from the left.

Showing their diminished influence, the *Judge*, *Victim* and *Ego* are all lighter in color and intensity as it diminishes in solidity. The *Red Arrows* of *Desire* have dramatically reduced in number and strength of color.

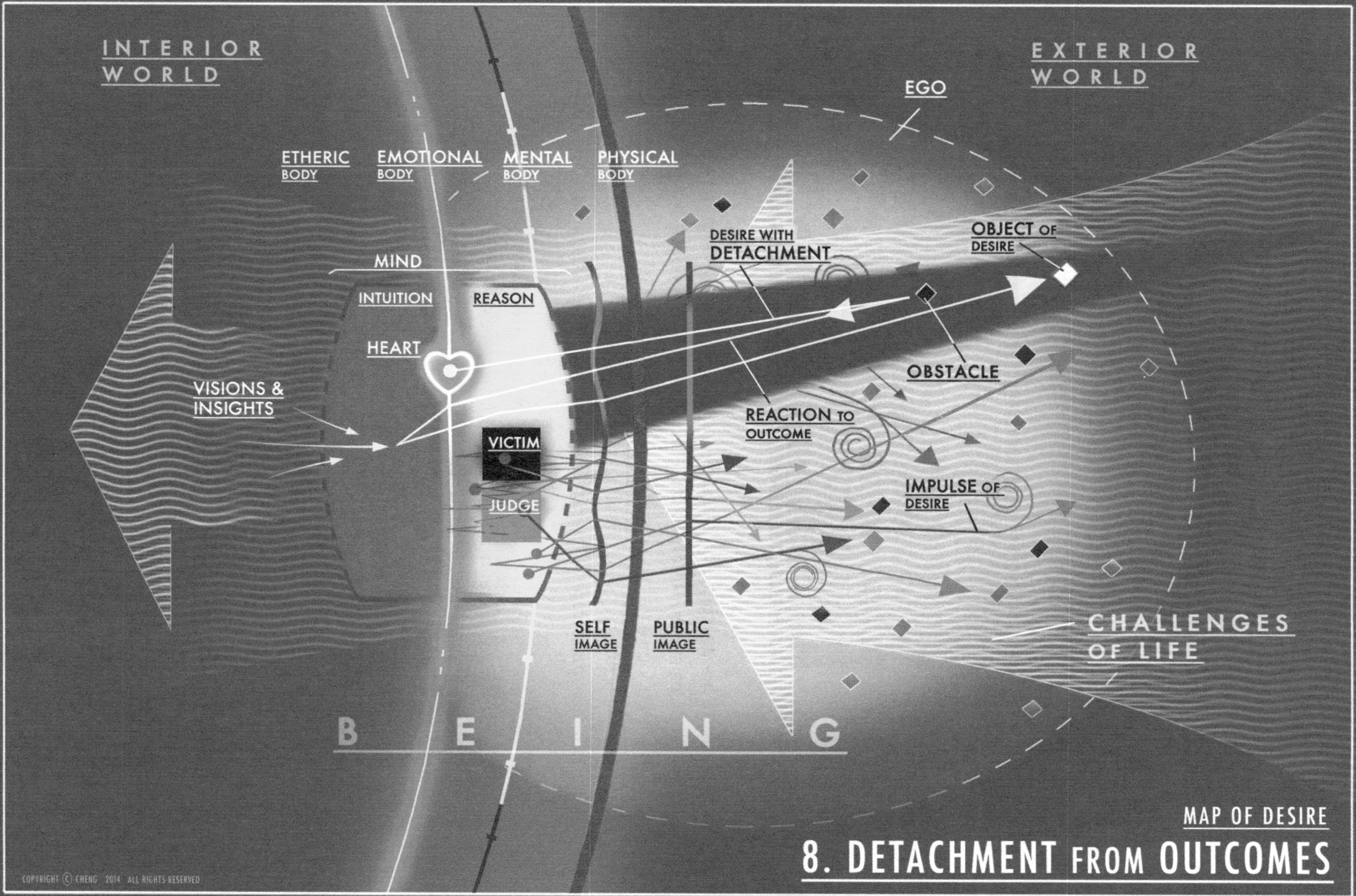

INTERIOR
WORLD

ETHERIC
BODY

EMOTIONAL
BODY

MENTAL
BODY

PHYSICAL
BODY

MIND

INTUITION

REASON

HEART

VISIONS &
INSIGHTS

VICTIM

JUDGE

SELF
IMAGE

PUBLIC
IMAGE

B E I N G

DESIRE WITH
DETACHMENT

REACTION TO
OUTCOME

OBSTACLE

IMPULSE OF
DESIRE

OBJECT OF
DESIRE

EGO

EXTERIOR
WORLD

CHALLENGES
OF LIFE

MAP OF DESIRE

8. DETACHMENT FROM OUTCOMES

What is detachment?

With detachment, we become free of so much of the clamor out in the world (and within ourselves) that we can't help but gain a new lightness of being. Even though there will always be drama in the world—political upheavals, financial downturns, earthquakes, death in the family—our suffering still arises from our own reactions to the drama. It's not what happens to us that causes our grief, but rather, how we choose to respond to situations. As Shakespeare puts it, "Nothing is good or bad; only thinking makes it so."

> *Detachment from outcomes*
> *Amidst the carnival of strife*
> *Aims our attention once more to the Now,*
> *engaging our will at the root of all life.*

Detachment frees us from expectations and assumptions. When dominated by the ego, we crave control, and routinely become troubled when events don't unfold according to plan. Thwarted, our ego-driven self immediately wants to find someone to blame (quite often ourselves), justify its own faults, and defend its precious opinions, all of which cost a tremendous expenditure of energy over nothing but a false expectation.

Public Image
No distortion interacting with the public.

In Map 8, the white arrow of desire shows no distortion as it crosses the green line of *Public Image* because it has become straight. With freedom from expectations, there is no need to fabricate a false public persona to impress the vagaries of the world. Detachment recognizes that sooner or later, following natural law, everything of the visible world passes, and often changes to their opposite, so why cling to anything so ephemeral? (The classic Taoist Yin-Yang symbol expresses this reality with a dot of Yin in the midst of Yang, and vice versa.) So, freed from fears of losing what we have, or anxiety over an uncertain future, or misgivings from the past, detachment leaves us in the eternal present... grateful to be alive.

On a subtle level, detachment also recognizes that the *results* of what we do, not to mention all the possessions in our life, (including our bodies, houses, jobs, children, victories, sorrows, and opinions), ultimately, *do not belong to us*. They are not our essence, not who we really are. We are more glorious than all our deeds or accomplishments combined.

We deal with our body, house and jobs, of course, and deal with them well—they are what we've been calling our "secondary objectives,"—but, as we have seen, their true value can only be seen in how they affected our "primary objectives," how much true love, wisdom, and joy we have extract from them.

A Tibetan monk who had vowed to remain in his cave until he became enlightened was asked during a workshop in California how he felt when the Chinese invasion forced him to leave his home. Through a translator, he answered that he felt bad; because of his "bad karma," he was forced to break his vow. On the other hand, he told us, he felt fortunate; because of his "good karma," he was allowed to travel through Europe, America, and see the richness of the world. Everyone was struck not only by his aura of peace in spite of his travails, but also his level of detachment that allowed him to be free from even his own "good" and "bad" karma.

Detachment does *not* mean that you don't care, because you most certainly do. Actually, you'll be caring at a much deeper and more effective level because your concerns now include not only the effects, but also their causes. Whatever the situation, you will take appropriate action as best as you can. *Internally,* however, you accept *what is* while remaining free of the usual mind chatter filled with doubts, accusations, and worries. Coupled with the preceding Map 7, **Attunement to Being**, you will know to lay aside your ego's idea of what, when, and how something should happen, and allow Spirit to take charge.

In Map 8, **Detachment from Outcomes**, the white arrow—representing a desire with "detachment to outcome"—again launches from the *Heart* and shoots through the yellow territory of ego directly towards its goal. When its path is blocked by the Obstacle, its return path, *Reaction to Outcome,* shows minimal "Bounce-Back" between elements of the ego. This is because detachment makes us free of how our efforts are received by the outside world.

Benefits from detachment

A major blessing that comes with detachment is freedom from the conventions of society or dictates of parents or peers. *No longer does your fulfillment depend on anything outside of yourself.* Whether complimentary or critical, the need for outside approval or acknowledgement is no longer central to your well-being. So many desires aimed at keeping up impressions or worrying about what people may think are now seen to be unnecessary, irrelevant, ludicrous. You are free.

Peace of mind unshaken by adversity is another benefit that comes from detachment. How many of us have experienced tremendous anxiety from setbacks only to realize in retrospect that they were blessings in disguise. If you can remain centered in spite of victories or defeats, you gain *equanimity.* You're able to take everything in stride, accept *what is—love* what is—and remain open as to how Spirit brings her gifts to you.

A third benefit of detachment is patience. Allowing life to bring her treasures to you at her own pace instead of the ego's timetable of expectations requires patience. An example of this can be seen in football games: a running back does not always simply charge forward with the ball. Often times, he would patiently run in place for a few seconds until his blockers have time to open up a hole through the defense. Then, and only then will he shoot through to gain his yardage. How important it is have patience in creative projects so that you're free from feeling rushed as you respect the process of the projects unfolding. You can't yank a plant up to make it grow faster. With patience, you gain the faith that *What is truly yours, will surely come.*

These benefits gained from detachment of fulfillment, equanimity, and patience greatly reduce the chaos of your desires. Instead of blindly hungering for more at the first sign of anxiety, you can accept *what is* and give space to let events unfold at their own good time. (Practical exercises to experience these benefits can be found at the end of this book under *Practices.*)

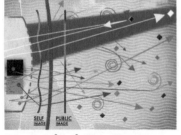

Diminished Ego Desires
Lessening selfish wounds.

In Map 8, the benefits mentioned above can be seen through the red arrows of desires, which have greatly reduced not only in number but also in intensity. Though old, ego-driven desires still linger, they are no longer a driving force with which we pin our hopes for fulfillment.

Detachment in daily life

To bring detachment into daily life, one of the first things you can do is to be a *master of your own attention*. Where your attention is placed is where your life-force is spent, and where it is spent is where things will grow. To conserve and build the energy for your heart's desire, your attention is not to be squandered blindly. When you master your own attention there is no waste of *chi* on assumptions, cynicism, outcomes, junk media, meaningless arguments, and gossip.

For example, a friend of mine became infuriated and cynical with the news:

"Same old thing, it's been going on for years."

"Well, if it gets you so angry, why do you watch it?"

"I have to know what's going on. Be informed."

"But you already know. Like you said, it's the same old thing."

At this point, my friend could choose to "master his attention" by withdrawing it from the news, and placing it on something inspiring. He could still occasionally scan the papers and/or TV for anything different, truly informative or uplifting. By so doing, he could save himself a lot of needless anger and cynicism.

In Map 8, this focused attention is seen with the clear, true path of the white arrow. With unbending intent, the arrow goes for its mark, gets blocked, reassesses, and simply goes for its mark again. The arrow shows its clarity of intent by what it has avoided (the Judge and the Victim) as much as what it remains focused upon (its goal).

Be in the moment

A powerful way to practice detachment is to *be in the moment*. When you are in the moment, you can once again feel the joy of being totally immersed in whatever you are doing free of the burdens from the past or worries of the future. This is your natural state, the way you lived when you were a child. Filled with pleasure that comes when you are totally in the present, your means and ends become one.

> *Detachment returns to us the great gift of doing*
> *No more worrying over what might be lost or won.*
> *Just beyond seductions of "success,"*
> *in all endeavors, means and ends are one.*

In Zen practice, to be in the moment gives one the experience of "beginner's mind" when all is experienced fresh and new and the most mundane activity can become an opportunity for self-liberation. Thus we have the Zen of "flower arrangement," of "archery," of "washing dishes," and of "experiencing sorrow" The ego, of course wants to put a judgment on everything—"*This* is important, that is not..."—but with no judgment or attachment every activity becomes unique and freshly experienced.

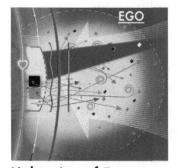

Lightening of Ego
Shifting focus to higher powers.

In Map 8, the reduction of the power of ego is shown through its color, which has shifted from an intense, deep orange (as seen in Map 6) to light yellow. The ego's materiality has diminished, and its edges have become transparent as it is increasingly revealed to be an illusion with no solidity.

Do your best, leave the rest

To become truly detached, you want to do your best in any situation. When you know you've done your best you can relax knowing that what comes or doesn't come is no longer your concern. *Do your best, and leave the rest.*

However, whether from laziness, doubt, or lack of courage, if you *don't* do your best you open yourself to regret and will not be able to practice detachment. Your inner critic, ever ready to judge you for shortcomings or setbacks, real or imagined, will jump at you from inside and sabotage your faith and confidence.

The "best" is not to be confused with your ego's (or your parents, peers, or media's) idealistic fantasy of perfection. That would be *more* than your best, another trap, an impossibility to live up to and a cause for needless suffering.

How, then, do we know what is our best? Don't we often want to grow by going past our comfort zone? Yes, of course. Ultimately, your feelings will tell you when you've done your best. If you worked hard pushing yourself beyond your norm until you're fatigued but still feel happy, then you would have pushed the boundaries of your personal best without going overboard.

However, when the same activity feels like "work" and you feel heavy, resentful, or *obligated* to push on—here is when "stupid mistakes" begin to appear—it's a sure sign that you're going beyond your best, and that it's time to stop and take a break.

In Map 8, to represent actions when we are "doing our best," we see the white arrow labeled *Reaction to Outcome* bypass the Judge and Victim because we are free of self-incrimination and feelings of victimhood. The "Bounce-Back" denoting reactions to outcomes, thus remain minimal.

Surrender to *what is*
The ultimate way to practice detachment is to surrender to *what is* with no resistance. Whether a result seems to be a triumph or a tragedy, we know it is only an appearance, a temporary situation that will shift continuously. Even our own feelings—grief, despair, anger—we accept and surrender with no judgment. We're allowed our feelings. They don't need to be justified. The challenge is to experience our emotions while remaining free of the ego's tendency to pass judgments or to create rationales and justifications. We will delve into this at more length in the next chapter.

Whatever the desire or goal, move towards it knowing that *how* you move forward—with passion, commitment, and detachment—is every bit as important as *what* you do. Do the "ends justify the means?" No. Are the "ends," then, of no importance? No, again. The *process and the goal are one.* Gandhi's famous statement, *"Be the peace you want in the world,"* is a great expression of how the means and ends are one.

"Surrender" does *not* mean you become completely passive to life. If you're in the midst of a difficult predicament—your car running out of gas on the freeway—you do *not* throw up your hands, declare that you are in surrender mode, and do nothing but sit there. It is an *inner* surrender you hold to. You could complain and judge the situation—"My wife should have filled the gas tank after she used it," or "Why does this always happen to me?" or "I hate driving, I hate the city, I hate not having public transit…" Instead, accept *inwardly* what has fallen onto your path even as you take action to remedy the outer situation as best as you can (if necessary or possible). In this case, simply get more gas.

Here in <u>Map 8,</u> surrendering to *what is* permits the white arrow to remain straight and true and its *Reaction to Outcome* to be direct and simple. It should be clear by now that the more we evolve in consciousness, the simpler life becomes. As we saw earlier, we find that though we perform less, we accomplish more.

> *Pure passion, innocent of expectation*
> *Lusts no longer take their toll.*
> *Fulfillment rides on nothing outside of ourselves*
> *failure cannot exist in the realm of the soul.*

Attunement to Being reconnects us with the infinite power of our Source, and **Detachment from Outcome** frees us from entanglements with a fickle and delusionary world. At this point, the only possible obstacle to personal freedom comes from *within ourselves* through personal wounds. These, we will address in the next chapter.

* * *

9. HEALING THE WOUNDS

Our heart glows, and secret unrest
gnaws at the root of our being.

—Carl Jung

Filling the hole in the heart

We now come to the last of the "three clear paths" that can lead us to personal freedom. If *Attunement to Being* connects us to our Source in Spirit, and *Detachment from Outcomes* frees us from the illusions of the outside world of appearances, we're left with the last of the major paths towards freedom—*Healing the Wounds*. Here, we focus on personal demons that torment us from within.

Psychological wounds such as mistrust, anxiety, fears, and judgment can be seen as "holes in our heart" of which judgment is the most damaging. Having endured such wounds for so long, we assume that they're a part of life, and repress them so that we can soldier on with our worldly responsibilities.

Though we may have been effective in denying them, they're often revealed when even the slightest provocation—a contradictory opinion, a snide remark, a sinkful of dishes—causes an explosion of rage, self-loathing, or black depression. Venting our emotional pain, many of us automatically blame the outside world for all our torments, oblivious to the true source of our distress…the hole in our heart, a wound within.

However, once we *do* heal our wounds, everything changes. No more pain. No more judgment or self-pity. We feel clean inside and can rediscover the wild wonder we felt as a child when the world was our toy to explore. But first things first; we must brace ourselves and prepare to confront the most daunting of foes, our own inner demons. Here, then is Map 9, *Healing the Wounds.*

LEGEND · PART THREE : THE WAY OUT

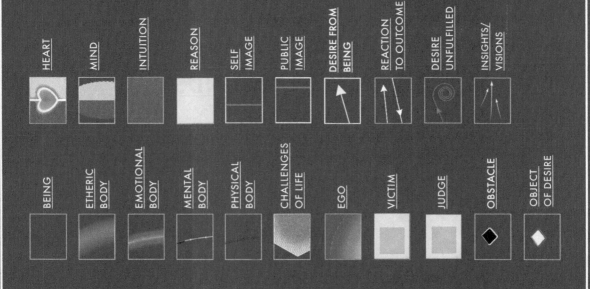

HEART · MIND · INTUITION · REASON · SELF IMAGE · PUBLIC IMAGE · DESIRE FROM BEING · REACTION TO OUTCOME · DESIRE UNFULFILLED · INSIGHTS/ VISIONS

BEING · ETHERIC BODY · EMOTIONAL BODY · MENTAL BODY · PHYSICAL BODY · CHALLENGES OF LIFE · EGO · VICTIM · JUDGE · OBSTACLE · OBJECT OF DESIRE

Map 9: HEALING THE WOUNDS

In this map, the thick, white arrow represents a desire free of unhealed wounds. Launched from the *Heart*, it traverses a direct path towards its *Object of Desire*. The green lines of the *Self* and *Public Image* (both now straight) no longer distort its trajectory.

However, when its progress is thwarted by the *Obstacle*, the thin, white arrow labeled *Reaction to Outcome*, remains simple and direct with minimal "Bounce-Back" between elements of the Ego. Its path includes entry into the purple area of *Intuition* allowing access to *Visions* and *Insights*, as represented by the three small arrows coming from the left.

Representing their reduced influence, the colors of the *Judge* and *Victim* have again diminished in intensity, while the *Ego* has lost even more of its solidity. The red arrows of desire have further decreased in number and potency in color.

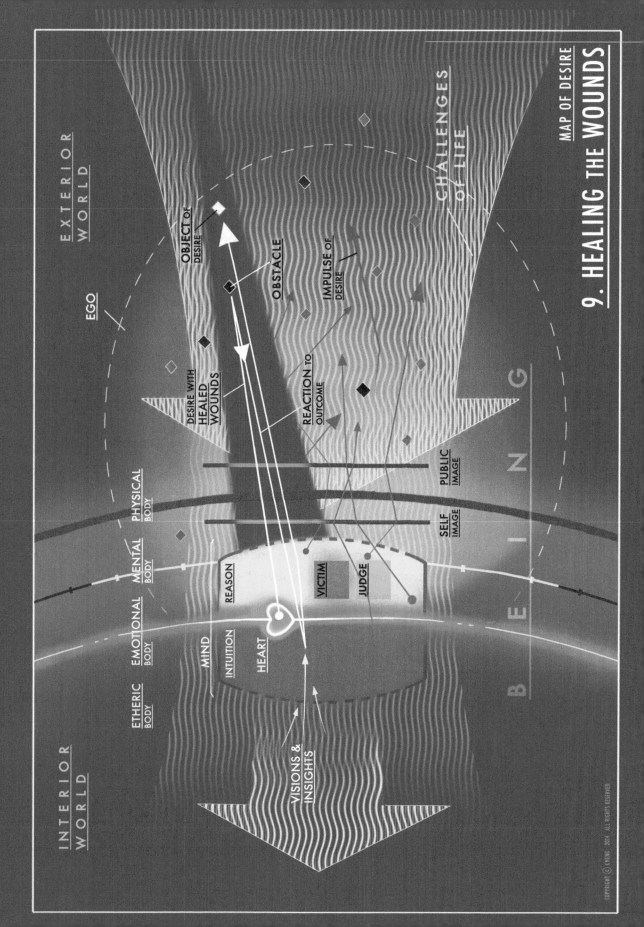

INTERIOR
WORLD

EXTERIOR
WORLD

EGO

ETHERIC
BODY

EMOTIONAL
BODY

MENTAL
BODY

PHYSICAL
BODY

MIND

INTUITION

REASON

HEART

VICTIM

JUDGE

SELF
IMAGE

PUBLIC
IMAGE

VISIONS &
INSIGHTS

DESIRE WITH
HEALED
WOUNDS

OBJECT OF
DESIRE

OBSTACLE

IMPULSE OF
DESIRE

REACTION TO
OUTCOME

CHALLENGES
OF LIFE

B E I N G

MAP OF DESIRE

9. HEALING THE WOUNDS

> *Who dares face that ancient fortress?*
> *The secret siege that's defined us for years.*
> *Who dares breach the gates, naked and unarmed,*
> *to jump down the well of sorrow and fears?*

Facing your wounds

Addressing your own wounds requires a special kind of warriorship. You assume responsibility for your own life including your own pain. No more do you blame the exterior world for your misgivings. If something irritates you, you ask, "What's *my* part in this angst? How is my interpretation of events causing my own demise?" If you don't like your predicament, you know to change your attitude—*thoughts take form*. No more will you be victimized by the outside world for you have chosen to take full responsibility for your own reality.

With this responsibility comes the need to know what's bothering you, what's keeping you back from fulfilling your dreams. Though the ego wants to blame the outside world, you know that the first place to look is within. In the vast majority of situations, your reaction is way more debilitating than the original difficulty. So much hinges on your attitude. For instance, if there were an earthquake, one man may see it as the wrath of God and tremble in constant fear; another may believe it's a part of nature's self-regulating intelligence and take it all in stride. Your choice.

If you remain oblivious to your own inner workings, you will harbor debilitating beliefs and psychological patterns that can torture you for years with no clue that you are the source of your own demise. Unfortunately, most people suffer needlessly because of just this blindness. Unaware that they have the power to uplift their lives, they waste their *chi* blaming something outside of themselves for their problems.

For example, a man I know had been constantly shamed as a child by his father, "I love my son, really, but what a screw up…!" Thirty years later, well after his father had died, he still carried that humiliation by beating himself up. He became aware of this when he tried to justify a financial loss to his wife by blurting out, "I am who I am, okay? A screw up!" His wife challenged him directly, "Why do you say that? You're not a screw-up. Would I marry a screw-up? You're not a screw-up!" This exchange inspired him to seek the source of this belief until he remembered how his beloved father used to (inadvertently) humiliate him. It was just a "thought-packet" carried over from years before—a memory, a phantom, a virtual reality, nothing. Why is he still hanging on to it?

Occurring unconsciously, these pains are insidious because their causes are so well hidden they make you think it is a part of life. If these wounds are not faced, they'll naturally cause you years of fears and pains. If still ignored, they'll reveal themselves as chronic backaches, ulcers, and other physical ailments.

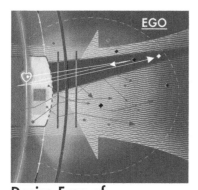

Desire Free of Unhealed Wounds
No more distortions from inner demons.

It is instructional to compare this Map 9 with Map 6, *Tyranny of Desire* with its overwhelming mass of red arrows of desire. The arrows of desire in the second map come in large part from a desperate attempt to alleviate inner pains through something outside of us. By contrast, in the map of this chapter the feeling tone is lighter, the *Ego* is transparent, and the thicket of red arrows of desires has greatly diminished in number and depth of color.

Hole in the Heart

In the shamanic tradition, these hidden but debilitating thought patterns are seen as *parasites.* They are considered living non-physical entities that feed on one's emotions. Carl Jung called them "the shadow." He urged individuals, as well as humanity, to face these dark, unsavory aspects hidden in our unconscious. Joseph Campbell spoke of them as the "hidden movers," the ultimate enemy the hero must confront on his transformational journey. In Zen practice, the willingness to face this shadow side of ourselves (and of life) is called "eating bitter," and is essential on the path to liberation.

Whatever these "demons" are called, most people remain oblivious to them and routinely deny their source—their own "hole in the heart." No matter how much outer achievement they may have, no matter how far up the ladder of success they've climbed, they can never run far enough away from that hole in the heart, and so they suffer. Even when exposed, denial and rationalizations from the ego shove these demons back into the shadows since most people prefer to endure customary torments rather than break out into the unknown territory called peace and fulfillment.

This pattern is illustrated by the example of a famous actor who was one of the stars in a movie that won "Best Picture" in the Academy Awards. He was a true artist and had "everything going for him," (at least in the conventional sense)—talent, wealth and fame. At the height of his stardom, contrary to character, he suddenly began making irrational decisions and speaking so caustically to those around him that he undermined his own stardom. "You can't trust the world," he said. "When youth and beauty fade, they throw you away like a used Kleenex." The hole in his heart welled up from a deep and private sorrow—he was given away to an institution as a child. But under the glare of the limelight, no way could he tend to this issue. His antagonistic actions led to a self-fulfilling prophecy, which resulted in more abandonment. No one would work with him anymore because he was too belligerent on the set. This unfortunate story reveals the insidious power of the parasite to sabotage from within.

The actor had worked hard and long to become a movie star because he wanted to be loved and accepted. Once this goal was achieved, his initial desire multiplied into a dozen more—custom tailored suits, late-model cars, Malibu address, all of which contributed to his increasing confusion because all that he thought he wanted was not making him happy. It had been sabotaged by his inner demons. Such an inner state of mind is illustrated by Map 6, *Tyranny of Desire* with its chaotic thicket of red arrows of desire.

If he had looked within and healed his wounds—if he could have received some guidance like Alicia had gotten from her father—he could have saved years and years of unfulfilling effort, greatly simplified his life and found happiness as an artist. This state of mind can be seen in this Map 9, *Healing the Wounds*. You'll notice that the entire image is simpler and lighter, a sharp contrast to Map 6, *Tyranny of Desire* mentioned above.

Phantom demons

In Map 5, *Formation of Ego*, we discussed two of the most debilitating of our many demons, the *Judge* and the *Victim*. The Judge blames everyone and everything for whatever ego deems unsatisfactory, reserving his most severe judgments on...ourselves. Over and over again, we are found guilty. The Victim wraps us in self-pity, often rendering us powerless. Typically set in place during early years of childhood, our inner Judge and Victim perpetuate these patterns of accusations and condemnations (like the example of the man who saw himself as a "screw up") long after we've left home. They've become so chronic and familiar that they become part of the fabric of our identity.

Although we have endured untold suffering from these inner demons for years, we keep them alive by feeding them our attention. We believe in them. We believe in them even though they have continually chastised us, "You're not good enough." "Why are you such a wimp?" "Why aren't you married by now?" No one forces us to continue listening to these demons except blind habit and ignorance. They are nothing but mere thought-form phantoms, mental constructs, soap bubbles...unreal.

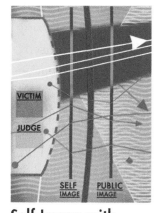

Self Image with No Distortion
Desires free of judgment or delusions.

In Map 9, the drastic simplification of the white arrow (compared to the red arrows of Map 6, *Tyranny of Desire*) is a sign of someone who has seen through the illusion of the ego's desires. Having addressed her own inner demons, she becomes free of pain, and the world is seen anew. Her desires now come from the heart and feed her soul, hence the white arrow. (Again, for specific exercises to address the inner Judge and Victim, see *Practices* at the end of this book.)

Benefits from healing the wounds

When you address your wounds at their source *within*, you begin healing your emotional and psychological pains. The benefit: No more suffering, anxieties or fears!

What's more, you no longer need to blame the outside world for your troubles and woes. This saves a tremendous amount of *chi* usually spent covering up humiliations, failures, and private suffering. This energy can then be re–deployed for fulfilling your dreams. The *chi* you'll save! Free of pain, your perceptions regain clarity and your activities once again become enjoyable.

In Map 9, this healing of the wounds is shown in the green line depicting *Self Image*. Similar to the line for *Public Image,* it is now straight and no longer distorts your desires since you are free of self-delusion. There is nothing more to cover up. Free of the illusion that your wounds can be healed from anything outside of yourself, there are fewer red arrows of desire.

The eternal now
Having healed your wounds, you can once again experience the "eternal now." You are free of your Judge and the Victim and their mental constructs that are invariably tied to grievances from the past or worries about the future. You are liberated from the illusion of time, and each moment can unfold in the magic of the present.

By now, you understand that *everything is temporary*. You could even "enjoy" setbacks, and practice the "Zen of disappointment" knowing that disenchantments come and go and are part of the game of life.

As wounds heal, you free yourself of judgments, cynicism, pet peeves, guilt and all manners of discomfort. You trust life again to be what it is instead of clinging to the ego's tyrannical demands of what it *should* be. Daily life becomes an adventure and a blessing. Even with responsibilities as adults, you regain your original, childlike sense of discovery and joy. As you practice healing your wounds—five steps forward, three steps back—you can enjoy the process as you would a challenging game.

In Map 9, **Healing the Wounds**, the *Ego* has greatly diminished in color and intensity because living in the present cuts through the ego's dependency on past and future. Likewise, the colors and intensity of the Judge and Victim are greatly reduced, reflecting their diminished influence on the individual. This new clarity is expressed through the increasing serenity and simplicity of the blueprint. What is *not* there is as important as what is.

> *The mystery path winds through our wounds,*
> *Funding fortitude and faith 'long the way.*
> *Five steps forward, three steps back*
>   *the dance turns our trials into play.*

Healing the wounds in daily practice

What can we do on a practical level to heal our wounds? First admit that they exist. In the shamanic tradition, *Mastery of Awareness* is the first and most challenging step. It requires courage to look within since to peer into your own shadow side, all the qualities that you've been desperately trying to hide such as cowardliness, pettiness, and shame are revealed. It is no surprise that so many people shun psychological work. They may even lash out derisively—"I'm in the real world. Too busy to indulge in all that airy psycho babble"—because they know instinctively that all their weaknesses will be revealed. Yet this is where true healing begins.

Awareness allows you to see that suffering invariably comes from believing your own negative thought patterns; it is not situations per se that make you upset, but your thoughts and judgments about them. Once you confront these patterns, they dissolve and lose their hold on you because you can see that they are only "mental constructs, phantoms, soap bubbles...unreal."

If you take that unflinching look within, you may also see a glorious potential within. Nobility, secret dreams, and visions of such greatness that most of us don't dare speak them out loud can now become revealed. In our cynical society, who dares to risk humiliation by declaring their aspirations of greatness and glory? With newfound awareness, however, you can see with no false pride and no false modesty the potential of your magnificence. You have no idea of what you can become. These maps can help you claim your birthright. As the Bible declares, "The kingdom of heaven is within you." It is. Claim it. It's yours.

Map 9 shows the increasing directness and simplicity of the white arrows as a reflection of the growing awareness of what lies within. With minimum effort, they reach their

Objects of Desire, now colored white to depict goals attuned to Being. Time and again, from here on out, life as reflected in these maps becomes increasingly simple and direct.

Stalking our demons

We know that demons like our Judge and Victim have been lurking in our blind spots wreaking havoc from within us for years. How do we find them? For centuries, seekers throughout the world went on fasts and meditation retreats to flush out these saboteurs. To our day, these methods are still effective.

In recognition to our busy pace of life, however, there are more direct techniques to reveal your inner saboteurs. One easy way to track them down is by paying attention to *anything that upsets you.* For example in something as common as…pet peeves; big things are revealed in tiny ways. If certain situations make you bristle in anger—someone challenging your opinion, someone being late all the time, or interrupting you when you talk—you can be sure that a wound has been touched. You might think that when your opinions are challenged *you* are being attacked; or when someone is late, *you* are being disrespected. Taking things personally makes you so sensitive that the most offhand statement—"You gaining weight?" or "Are you in over your head?"—could trigger an emotional explosion, Boom!

A comparison of the lightness and simplicity of Map 9, *Healing the Wounds*, with Map 6, *Tyranny of Desire*, best illustrates the newfound freedom from such negative thought patterns.

Growing awareness enables you to change your behavior. When you begin to feel an emotional outburst brewing, instead of reacting in anger like usual, seize the opportunity to follow the trail to your inner saboteur. Like master hunters who track their prey, you stalk your demons by being alert to any clues of their whereabouts—pet peeves in this case—that allows you to follow them to their secret watering hole, your open wound, your "hole in the heart."

Gigi awakens

A client of mine whom I'll call Gigi endured a terrible divorce from her husband, Joe. An MTV Executive, he was filled with power and charm, and could tell the most beautiful, convincing lies. After years fighting as a couple, including three years in marriage, she spent the next seven years trying to divorce him. But he continually sabotaged the proceedings as a ruse to avoid paying her settlement. How she suffered through his mendacity and abuse! And how she lost years of her life trying to end her entanglement.

During a shamanic workshop, she complained bitterly of how he had repeatedly lied and cheated on her. She spoke of incidents that further revealed his vindictive nature. Naturally, the question came up, "Why did you marry him? After those countless lies, weren't you wary of his character before you married him?" She was not. Even when she caught glimmers of his true nature, she would remain enamored by his charm. She suppressed her own insights and tried to "make things better."

"I wanted to trust him. Give him a chance," she replied.

"But you didn't trust him," I said. "You didn't trust him to be who he is, a pathological liar. Instead, you only trusted your idealized version of what you thought he should be and tried to change him accordingly. But of course, it never worked, and you're still entangled."

From here, we traced the first time that she felt so victimized. Through painful tears, we uncovered a deep and painful memory of how her stepfather had abused her sexually when she was a young teenager. When she finally had the courage to tell her mother, her mother sided with the stepfather, who even accused Gigi of wrongdoing for the gall of seducing him! Both parents chastised her severely for lying. From then on, she never brought up the subject again. She had *lost faith in her own perceptions*, an injury that proved much more damaging than the rape.

In the thirty years since then, this pattern of being victimized by colleagues, lovers, and neighbors would frequently haunt her, including her choice to marry Joe. Once, when their marriage was starting to unravel, Joe had amused dinner friends with an idea for a TV show, "Wouldn't it be fun to create a game show called "Getting Revenge on Your Ex?" Everyone laughed, how cynically chic! But Gigi was horrified. That moment revealed a troubling insight about Joe. She must leave him right away, she told herself. But the next moment, she explained it away, and even turned on herself, "Lighten up. Why are you always so serious? He'll change." After what she had endured with her stepfather and mother, she considered abuse by her husband as part of normal life.

Map 6, *Tyranny of Desire* illustrates Gigi's situation with its wavy green lines of *Self* and *Public Image* that continually distorted her own insights, interactions and desires.

Distortions from Self and Public Image
Chaos from the unexamined self.

Now that her hidden wound was out in the open, Gigi could see the part *she* played in her present day conflicts. Sometimes, the slightest off-hand remark from someone would trigger an explosive reaction from her. As if possessed, she became an angry, accusatory, self-righteous hellcat and attacked friends and foes alike. It was a perfect match for her ex (who had his own combative issues). Together, they would engage in ferocious battles that eventually led to the divorce.

This hellcat part of her, she realized, was a sub-conscious re-action to the unaddressed rage caused by her sexual abuse. Though the rape had ended long ago, she still carried the belief that the world is filled with *people much more powerful than you who will abuse you, so don't ever speak out if you want to survive.* She saw her hellcat attacks as a desperate protest to address this wrong. This belief also allowed abusers and liars to intrude into her life and exploit her original wound, the "hole in her heart."

Now that she could face this thought-construct head-on, she understood that the conclusions she drew from the rape were *not* reality, but only an interpretation she had created during sensitive formative years. Finally, she could see a way out of this self-defeating pattern of not trusting her own conclusions and of believing she was a victim. It was only a description of a dream. It was not real. No longer did she need to waste personal power complaining about how this person or that institution had judged or victimized her. Rather, she could be vigilant against letting such old wounds come back into her life. By seeing the true source of her angst, she started to regain her power and let true healing begin.

Forgiveness
As anyone on the path knows, this kind of healing is not a linear process—five steps forward, three steps back. Such old wounds as Gigi's are deep-rooted. Though they will most certainly lessen, they may keep arising in spite of her new understanding. So how can we best deal with it? How can we wash ourselves clean of this emotional poison?

The ultimate cleansing of your emotional wounds is achieved through *forgiveness*. Forgive those who, in your eyes, wronged you—parents, lover, boss, or friend. (Quite often, they suffered the same abusive conditioning you had and like you, did the best they could at the time.) You might think it "cowardly" to forgive because it means that you're letting someone get away with something, but that's more of your ego's delusion. Rather, forgiveness is the most effective way to cleanse the poison out of your emotional body.

Gigi revealed her powers of forgiveness when, on the day of her divorce, she was able to tell her ex that though it was not right for them to remain married, she still loved him for who he truly was in spite of their differences. From then on, she felt decidedly lighter about her time with Joe.

This moment of forgiveness was a breakthrough for Gigi. Not only had she advanced a great step in dealing with her ex, but she had also moved forward in fulfilling her "primary purpose" of being on earth. In spite of her sufferings, *because* of her sufferings, she now saw that she was capable of granting unconditional love. She had gained an insight of knowing her true nature, of who she truly was.

You also want to forgive *yourself* for your shortcomings, real or imagined. No longer do you have to "beat yourself up," and suffer because of your own inner Judge and Victim. If past actions do not measure up to your present standards, you can promise yourself that you will do better next time. You understand that with the level of awareness that you had at that time, you did your best. With this knowledge, you can forgive yourself and drop your ego's tendency for self-judgment.

In Map 9, with no more self-delusion, the green line of *Self-Image* is now straight, and creates no distortion on the trajectory of the white arrow. The white line of the Bounce-Back enters the area of *Intuition* showing how we can now receive further insights on our predicaments as they arise in any life situation.

Feel the feelings, drop the stories

When we are struck by old negative emotions in our daily life, what's to be done? In Gigi's case the old patterns still came up, which is understandable considering they had been ingrained for over thirty years. The short answer: Feel the sorrow or anger, for sure; but drop the "stories." These stories come from the ego's inclination towards self-pity, blame, judgment, or justification for how you feel. Your emotions do not need to be justified. *Feel the feelings, drop the stories.*

To feel the feelings while sidestepping the thinking mind, sit quietly as if in meditation. Focus on how the emotions affect the body—the heaviness in the chest and the cringing in the stomach. Imagine the textures and colors of those feelings—dirty blue, hot red. Give them full attention while remaining free of the thinking mind. Watch how emotions, like water with no container, change and adapt to new situations. Anger might typically shift into sadness, sadness into compassion.

As children—before the intellect took over—we could be so angry one moment and five minutes later be happily playing with the very person who riled us in the first place. When mental constructs are released, emotions flow freely. For Gigi, whenever adversity struck, she applied her new vigilance against falling into old habits of victimhood. She categorically refused to let her thoughts run away with her, focusing instead on her feelings and remaining free of the "stories."

Just because we're on a spiritual path we are in no way pretending that we only feel wonderful. We want to feel everything, and deeply, even if those feelings are "negative" like anger, grief, fear and despair. By avoiding the accusations, self-pity, and justifications so prevalent with our thinking mind, we can then experience a fully-lived life.

To be clear, *thinking* that is essential to assess our situations should *not* be confused with the incessant mind chatter and knee-jerk judgments that can cause endless suffering. Once we understand our predicament, we can drop the endless thoughts that the ego loves to indulge in. (For specific exercises, please see *Practices* at the end of this book.

When we can *feel the feelings and drop the stories,* our lives become fully lived. Tragic or triumphant, we *feel* all our experiences, and can begin to appreciate the rich drama of being alive. We can then fulfill our primary cause by knowing how rich we are through all our life experiences.

> *Loose the grip of long-held habits*
> *Of insults, grudges, holy grails, and tired glories.*
> *From the echoes of a troubled past—*
> *feel the feelings, but drop the stories.*

In Map 9, the white arrow that begins in the *Heart* indicates emotional availability. The "Bounce-Back" enters the purple area of *Intuition*, which depicts access to intuitive insights. The slight bend in the yellow area of *Reason* shows distortion not from personal wounds, but from the intellect's ability to assess new situations and adjust trajectories accordingly.

Attunement to Being, Detachment from Outcomes, and ***Healing the Wounds*** can be practiced simultaneously, with each one greatly enhancing the effectiveness of the other two. Traversing these three pathways, we are well on our way to personal fulfillment. The next three maps will show stages of increasing freedom.

* * *

PART FOUR
TO FREEDOM

Having broken through the world of delusion, inside and out, our lives begin to fill with love, wisdom, creativity, and joy. These last three maps show the roadways of one enjoying increasing levels of personal freedom, and guide us towards the birthing of a new humanity.

10. MASTERY OF INTENT

I slept and dreamt that life was joy.
I awoke and saw that life was service.
I acted and behold, service was joy."

—Rabindranath Tagore

These final three maps show what happens when we practice the "three clear paths." Having broken through obstacles in the visible and invisible realms, we are increasingly free in our inner and outer world. Free of judgment or attachment, we live in harmony with the rhythms of the universe creating an electromagnetic force field around us of a heaven on earth. We think less and know more; we strive less, and accomplish more.

In the shamanic tradition, the word "intent" is a powerful term of mystery. In its highest meaning, it is synonymous with Spirit, God, Love, or Being. All these terms lose their distinction as we approach unity. In relation to the immensity of Spirit, how can we humans—time-bound, small, and uncertain as we are—make the connection? Through intent.

Intent has three requirements. It is…

- An impulse from the heart towards something bigger than our egos,
- A desire free of attachment to outcomes, and
- An action requiring that we do our best internally and externally.

These requirements are directly related to the last three maps (7, 8, 9) that showed us "the way out" to personal freedom. Map 10, *Mastery of Intent*, graphically depicts what it looks like to be a virtuoso in manifesting our dreams. As we wish, so we gain. Here, then, is a blueprint depicting that mastery…

Map 10: MASTERY OF INTENT

In *Mastery of Intent*, a white arrow, *Intent*, launches from the *Heart* shooting directly to its *Object of Desire*. Both *Self* and *Public Image* remain straight, and cause no distortions to its trajectory. There are no reactions or "Bounce-Back."

Representing their loss of influence, the colors and intensities of the *Ego, Judge* and *Victim* have so diminished that they are barely visible. There are no red arrows of desire and no "Obstacles" as before.

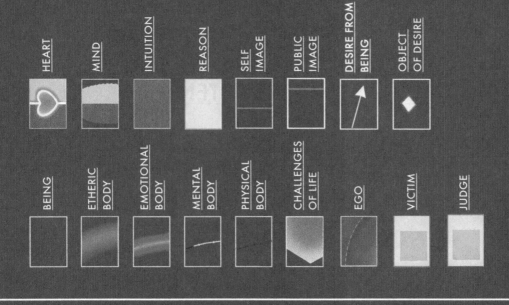

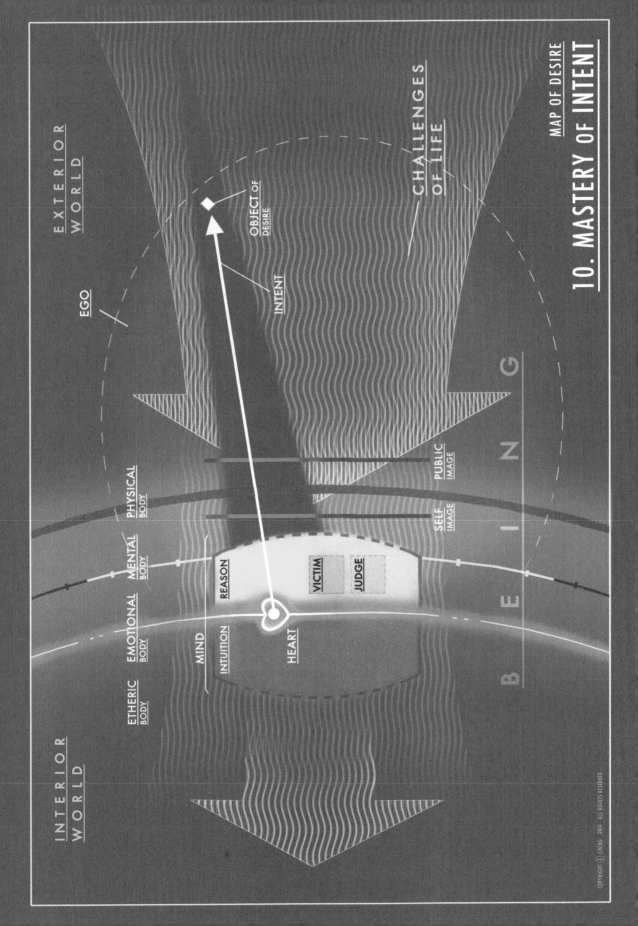

MAP OF DESIRE

10. MASTERY OF INTENT

Mastery of *intent*

The map shows that our actions as a Master of Intent are marked by simplicity, direct-ness, and power. All our undertakings are in service to a greater good; our will is at one with that of the universe. Free of the restraints and approval by a fickle public, we can act according to impulses from our heart. Our thoughts, words, and deeds are in agreement, which, like a laser beam, gives us power from a coordinated focus.

> *A Master of Intent co-creates the world,*
> *Mischief in his heart, thunderbolt in hand*
> *Image breaker, catalyst, co-conspirator on earth*
> *manifesting truth for a troubled land.*

In all we do, keep faith that *what's truly yours will surely come.* Declaring your intent, take action and simply witness what happens. With complete detachment, enjoy watching life move through you to unfold what you had intended… or not. Being detached and having done your best, you can accept that whatever happens does so in accordance to a higher authority.

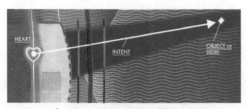

Desire from a Master of Intent
Clear, focused and powerful.

Map 10, *Mastery of Intent*, shows these vari-ous aspects of intent with a single white arrow that directly attains its goal. Launched from the *Heart,* it aspires to something beyond the do-main of ego, now barely visible. Free from judg-ments, expectations or attachment, there are no "Bounce-Back" complications whatsoever.

Notice that the arrow indicates a direct attainment of its *Object of Desire* with a trajectory free of distortions by the *Judge, Victim, Self* and *Public Image.* The red arrows of desire, so prevalent in earlier maps, have disappeared having been deemed irrelevant or have been transformed into *intent.*

Likewise, the *Judge* and *Victim* barely exist. The function of the *Judge* has been transformed into a new role. Instead of passing judgments between "good and evil," it now serves to discern between "truth and illusion," between what feeds our ego and what feeds our soul, or simply between "what I like, and what I don't like." No judgment. The function of the *Victim*, too, has evolved from a holding tank for self-pity into a repository for forbearance and acceptance. The trace of ego that still persists allows the individual to remain on earth as a physical being.

Manifesting effortlessly

When you master *intent*, material and spiritual abundance seem to appear magically. With Spirit as the unseen partner with whom you co-create, "you'll perform less, but accomplish more." Often, you'll find that you can begin to communicate without the need for words and know without the need to think (*silent knowledge* say the shamans). Insights come to you spontaneously, intuitively.

Synchronicity and "lucky accidents" are no longer surprising, but a living reality. Faith increases, which increases your powers of manifestation. Even with the vicissitudes of daily life, you're surrounded by a lightness of heart. Bold visions come to you and with no false modesty or false pride, you feel confident—especially with Spirit as your co-creator—to develop and manifest projects to help make a difference in the world.

With thoughts, words and deeds so coherently in synch, the Master of Intent often attracts "super-ordinary powers" such as telepathy, visions, and powers that add to the ease in manifesting one's dreams. These come spontaneously from Spirit and are neither sought for nor avoided, and are never used for self-aggrandizement. (If you do, your co-creator, mighty Spirit, will notice that you're off–point, and can strike you down ferociously.)

Examples of such masters of intent can be seen aplenty through history. Often they were considered dangerous for daring to speak truth to power. Utterly detached from self-serving outcomes, they could boldly face the status quo and declare themselves with no restraint. Guided by forces larger than themselves, these Masters, from Socrates to Lao Tze, from Van Gogh to Einstein, were able to leave behind treasures that shook the world.

In Map 10, the action of a Master of Intent manifest their yearnings directly with unbending focus, as can be seen in the white arrow that traverses its path straight and true to hit its mark.

Loving *what is*

With mastery of intent, *love what is,* including everything under the sun, "positive or negative." By now, the world of outcomes and appearances—*Maya*, the Cosmic Illusion, of Vedanta philosophy—is known to be an apparition and no longer has you under its spell. You walk through the world as if it were a dream. It *is* a dream.

Free of judgment, fear, or desire, you can accept *what is.* Even in the midst of great adversity or injustice when you may not *like* what you see, you still remain centered. Like a master warrior, whether you choose to act or not, you have surrendered inwardly to *what is* with no judgment. All you are experiencing is part of the miraculous flow of life allowing you to *love* what is.

Taste of freedom

Seers and sages, as we have declared repeatedly here in these pages, remind us that our adventures on earth have a deep purpose beyond that of cultivating careers, families, or masterpieces—that of self-realization. By knowing who you truly are, you can fulfill the "primary cause" of your being on earth.

Having been tossed and turned by the vicissitudes of daily living, you've finally wakened from the "dream of the planet" to realize that you're much more than all the dramas of your life. You've been the dreamer behind these dreams, and what a fine dreamer you've been. For all these years, you took your fabrications to be real!

What can be done with all this freedom? Explore other realms? Help change the world? Drop out and be a recluse? It's your choice; you're free.

In Map 10, this freedom and acceptance of *Life* is shown by the absence of the red arrows of desire that used to flood our world. All our desires have turned into *intent,* which by definition is in synch with universe. Our creative partner in all we do is Spirit.

Taking action

With the mastery of intent, one who chooses to remain active in the world will "do without doing." Accomplishment in the world is no longer dependent on intense *effort*. Rather, attunement with all-powerful Being allows its supreme powers of manifestation to flow through you for the general good. You need only to declare your intent and witness the results. This is the wisdom in the Taoist expression, *Wu-Wei,* "not-doing." You're in the *Tao* with no resistance to *what is* as you flow with the way of the universe.

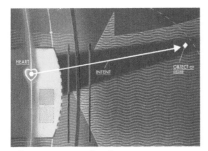

Flowing with the Universe
At one with what is.

In Map 10, the complete flowing "with the way of the universe" can be seen in the utter simplicity of the white arrow of *Intent*. The *Judge, Victim* and *Ego*, so light in color that they barely exist, no longer detract us from our source in Being and its capacity to materialize dreams.

One of the most esteemed and timeless of Hindu traditions, Vedanta philosophy, proclaims that one of the four major paths to enlightenment is through *Karma Yoga*, personal freedom through "God-dedicated action." For those who relish creating things in the world—artists, entrepreneurs, parents—it is heartening to know that through *action* one can find their union with Spirit.

However, there are three requirements. You must dedicate the fruits of your labor to God; be detached from results; and do your best, for it is God for whom you work.

Notice that these requirements are almost identical to our "three clear paths." One significant development is that with our maps here, we examine deeply the notion "do your best" by addressing the inner demons that prevent us from doing our best. "Doing your best" has been addressed on levels spiritually, psychologically and physically.

When we embark on these roads, we become part of a vast, unseen community devoted to self-fulfillment through these time-tested wisdoms that have fed everyone from Western Meso-American shamans to Eastern yogis and seers.

If we continue on our journey along these pathways, we enter an even more transcendent realm, which is the subject of the next map.

> *Spontaneous of action, heedless of fair praise*
> *Laughing at the limits of time and space,*
> *He walks among us, conjuring from folly*
> *mere treasures of wisdom and grace.*

* * *

11. BEYOND DESIRE

"Only he that rids himself forever of desire
can see the Secret Essences."

—Lao Tze

Beyond desire

Even though this book is a *Map of Desire,* we have come to a point where we've transcended desire. Free of ego and selfish yearnings, our aspirations have evolved into pure intent. This does not mean that we turn passive with no passion to act. As a matter of fact, we may be as profoundly active and productive as ever. Many evolved souls who have moved beyond (personal) desires have powerful, unbending intent. They build orphanages, write books, launch businesses, and transform countries. The key is that what we want is what Spirit wants. Our "secondary cause" is completely at one with our "primary cause."

At the same time, many who have evolved to this state of evolution may withdraw and appear to the outside world as unassuming, unimportant, or invisible. That does not mean, however, that they aren't helpful to the world. Instead of *doing,* they help by being, and radiate the quality of in-the-moment presence.

When we are beyond desire, we open to what is with no judgment, which allows Being to flow into all our actions. Life simply moves through us, or the way the poet Rimbaud put it, "I am the violin; God is the music." Map 11, *Beyond Desire,* pulls us back from the close-up of the preceding blueprints to see, once again, the whole picture…

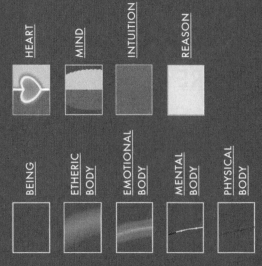

HEART

MIND

INTUITION

REASON

BEING

ETHERIC BODY

EMOTIONAL BODY

MENTAL BODY

PHYSICAL BODY

CHALLENGES OF LIFE

EGO

VICTIM

JUDGE

LEGEND . PART FOUR : FREEDOM

Map 11 : BEYOND DESIRE

Beyond Desire shows, once again, an overview of the *Human Form* floating in *Being*. The giant white arrow, *Challenges of Life*, continues its incessant flow through the individual, who, free of ego desire or attachment, has no more red arrows of desire. Like the preceding map, the *Ego, Judge* and *Victim* are barely visible.

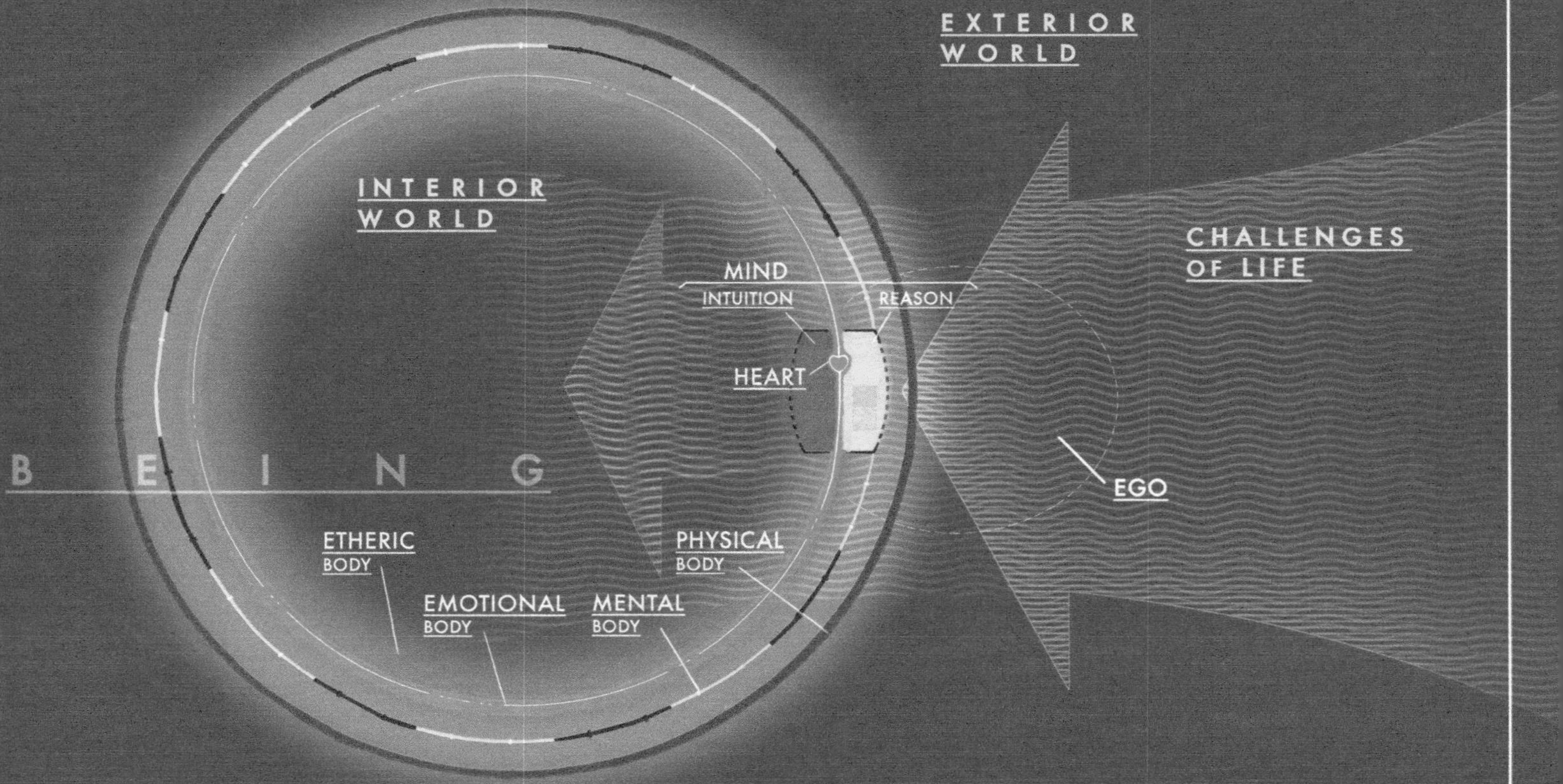

MAP OF DESIRE

11. BEYOND DESIRE

CHALLENGES OF LIFE

EXTERIOR WORLD

EGO

REASON

MIND
INTUITION

HEART

PHYSICAL BODY

MENTAL BODY

EMOTIONAL BODY

ETHERIC BODY

INTERIOR WORLD

B E I N G

In the map of this chapter, all the complexities of life have been pared to their essential simplicity. Living in the moment you have regained your innocence, your "beginner's mind." But this innocence does not mean that you're naïve. Picasso, for example, painted with the fresh, inventive candor of the innocent, but in no way was he naïve.

Meanwhile, the giant white arrow of the *Challenges of Life* continues to flow through you with no resistance or attachments from your part. Yet, if so inspired by an impulse from the heart, you know to seize your sliver of chance and spring into action as needed. And so you live at complete service to Spirit, backed by Spirit, co-creating with Spirit labors of love for the general good.

> *We have moved beyond desire,*
> *Acting only at the moment's command.*
> *Behold! Life's dramas ripple through us*
>   *serving all, though we but merely stand.*

Fragments of infinity

Up to this point, we have dealt with situations at the level of problems. Now, however, when you have moved beyond desire, you open yourself to the realm of *revelations*. Through powers of intuition and imagination, new worlds of possibilities open before you.

Just to be clear in speaking of imagination, we're *not* talking of idle daydreams, but rather of visions that can change your life, of fragments of infinity, of secrets of the universe. Here in the *imaginal* realm, you might see agreements made before you were born that reveal great insight for you in this life. Or perhaps you hover over planets of perfume with fragrances that make you feel young. Or by the light of a full moon, a jaguar leaps from your chest, and suddenly you know the direction of your next expansion.

Have you gone off the deep end? What's the limit?

There are no limits. You're in the imaginal realm. You *do* know how thoughts take form, so opening to Spirit, you trust your heart to guide your imagination, and witness startling results:

- You wake to the music of the morning of the world hearing harmonies that heal broken hearts,
- You feel rhythms in your head that can replace lost strands of our DNA,
- You see colors that inspire the transformation of tragedies into a new Golden Age!

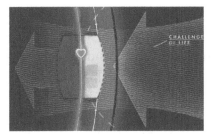

Freedom Beyond Desire
Life flows cleanly through you.

In Map 11, *Beyond Desire*, where are you? You can be anywhere in the blue area you want to be unbound by normal ego restraints. You are free. Will you get lost? No, because you are always linked to the everyday world through the powers of the *Heart*. So, with no fear or desire, watching, watching, you marvel at the flow of life moving through you.

As you free float in the imaginal realm, something demands your attention. With the panorama of infinite possibilities before you, you're pulled into an oasis with an electro-magnetic force field of harmony and peace. In its midst, you find *yourself* reading these words as you feel a gentle warmth on the back of your neck. You smile. You know that unseen eyes are looking after you, that you are being watched… by your Illumined Self, your "witness."

The witness

Yes, you are a multi-dimensional being. There is a part of you that can see your life as an outside observer, a *witness*. From this viewpoint, the adventures of your life are seen as a movie with yourself as the star. Sitting back, you enjoy the show, and laugh and cry at the foibles and breakthroughs of the hero. The ultimate "reality show." From the perspective of the witness, whatever happens has no real consequence to your well-being because it's all a movie. It's not the real you.

If you don't like the show, you can simply change the film and create a new intent. In shamanic practice, you would be "rewriting personal history." In normal life, you can revise the script, replace supporting characters and redesign sets to create new experiences and outcomes. Ever changing, ongoing, your life is indeed a movie. Whatever happens has got to be interesting. Or not. It's up to you. And in any case, it's just a movie.

But still, how grateful to be able to participate as a star in our own show! Equipped with a body, we can enjoy the rich sensations of the flesh and the sun, and all the passions of earthly life. At the same time, as multi-dimensional beings, we can also transcend physical life as a spirit being. From this viewpoint as that witness, we see clearly that *our _life_ is our greatest creation* and not our projects or possessions. We realize that *how* we play our roles is much more important than *what* that role happens to be. The only criteria for assessing the quality of our role-playing is, "Are we committed, passionate and heart-felt?" What happens or does not happen in our life is no longer our main concern, because from the perspective of Being, it's all a grand illusion.

Our destiny has been attained. Through the rich adventures of our "secondary causes," we have fulfilled our primary cause. We know who we are: God-filled multi-dimensional beings embodying mystery.

In Map 11, we are… off the map. As a witness, we are the one looking at the map seeing the whole movie of ourselves free–floating in a sea of infinity.

> *O, sacred imagination*
> *Too wildly profuse to ever still*
> *Visions upon visions, at one with all that's holy*
> *thoughts take form, according to her will.*

* * *

12. RETURN TO BEING

"O Nobly born, know thyself.
Thou art about to come face to face
with the clear light of pure reality."

—The Tibetan Book of the Dead

Coming home

With this last chapter, we've come full circle. Having experienced the richness of human possibilities with all its allure and entanglements, we've woken up! Filled with power, love, and joy, we know who we are. With one foot in the realm of the senses and the other in the Great Mystery, we've come home to Being, our Source and Essence.

Though we've come full circle, however, as with evolutionary cycles in nature, this circle is actually a spiral. We are at one with All That Is just as before when we were children, but this time we are *consciously aware* of who we truly are. Knowing this, we have fulfilled our destiny and live life with all the joy and opportunities that freedom can bring.

To be or not to be

Death does not exist. As sages and seers the world over have declared, "Yes, our bodies-will go, but consciousness remains eternal." Now we're at the point of another choice: Give up the body and dissolve back into our Source, the formless ocean of Love? Or, as stated in *The Tibetan Book of the Dead*, choose "rebirth and the seeking of the womb door?" Our choice. We're free.

This final Map 12, *Return to Being*, shows the last vestiges of the individual soul at the edge of the mystery poised between form and formlessness, to be or not to be...

LEGEND · PART FOUR : FREEDOM

Map 12: RETURN TO BEING

In *Return to Being*, the diaphanous ring of light of the *Etheric Body*, the human soul, floats in a field of infinite space in communion with eternal love, unlimited consciousness, and pure *Being*.

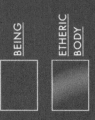

BEING

ETHERIC
BODY

B E I N G

> *Poised at the portal of Great Mystery*
> *I am that I am...*

Return to Being

This last map's simplicity depicts the situation for humans who have transcended time, space, and form. With joy within and without, we can dissolve into the ocean of infinity and feed on our own delight. Or...

Somewhere in the Mystery, an impulse ripples the ocean of Being, a desire, a vision, a soul seeks to be born...

> *Astride the ocean of infinity...I am.*
> *Whether as dreamer or dream...I am*
> *Long before a beginning...I am.*
> *and beyond the ultimate end...*

* * *

PRACTICES

Like quality maps and atlases that suggest scenic routes and excursions to enhance one's travels, we offer here *Practices* to enrich your journey towards self-fulfillment. For those seeking more than book-knowledge, these exercises allow one to gain *first-hand experience* of the benefits described in the text. They are tied in with the "three clear paths" of Chapters #7, #8, and #9.

Drawn from timeless wisdom traditions East and West, these exercises have been adapted to take in account our accelerated lifestyle. Honed and refined for more than twenty years through spiritual/shamanic workshops, they have proven most effective with seekers from all walks of life.

Here the real work begins. We're not saying it's easy. It may prove most challenging, but it's certainly achievable, and the pay-off is huge. Through practice, practice, practice, as artists, athletes, and yogis know, you can master any endeavor and set yourself free.

PRACTICES FOR
ATTUNEMENT WITH BEING

When we attune with Being, great power flows into our lives bringing insights, visions, compassion, and lucky "accidents." If these practices seem deceptively simple, it's because they defy our thinking mind; they're not to be *understood* so much as to be *experienced*. Magic happens when you attune to Being. Be ready.

COMMUNE WITH NATURE.

Nature is *Being* expressed in form. Our body knows its true mother, Mother Nature. Its essence of integrity, harmony, and balance are transmitted to us simply by spending time in natural environments.

1. Walk in nature, whether in the forest, beach or desert. Make it a regular activity, for example, once a week.
2. Maintain silence. Free yourself of the incessant activity of the thinking mind. Cherish the quiet mind.
3. Open your senses to the breeze on the skin, the sounds of leaves, and the infinite shades of color all around. Commune with the beauty before you, behind you, and all around.
4. If thoughts intrude, let them pass and refocus the attention on the rich sights, sounds and smells of nature.

As a tonic against the stress of daily life, you can find great comfort by walking among Grandfather Trees. You'll feel rejuvenated time and again simply by communing with nature.

HONOR WISDOMS OF THE BODY.

Our body has an "intelligence" of its own. Note, for instance, how our body performs the vast majority of its operations beautifully on its own. Its self-regulating, self-healing cells and organs masterfully communicate with each other. When we listen to our bodies, we tune into that inherent intelligence, and receive wisdom direct from our Source free of the distortions of the mind. Respect the wisdom of your physical form and you will receive benefits on all aspects of your life:

1. Be aware of signals from the body, such as the shiver up the spine, goose bumps on the arm, tightening in the stomach, or sudden sleepiness.

2. Be mindful of your last thought or activity before or during that bodily reaction. Typically, for example, many feel goose bumps when they're experiencing something they truly love, or gurgling in the stomach from anxiety, or heavy and dispirited after phone calls from certain people that drain their energy.

3. Trust your instincts. Make connections between your thoughts and bodily reactions. For example, let's say you are offered a job. You feel relieved because with the downturn in the economy, you can always use the money. But you also notice that you feel heavy and your stomach knots up as you think about that job. Your body may be revealing a conflict between your head and your heart: Deep down, you may not want to take it on. Though your head said *yes* (financial security), your heart said *no* (you have no respect for the purpose or the people connected with that job).

   Your body has exposed a deeper layer of truth. You can still decide either way on your course of action, but at least you know how you truly feel. (In general, though, always go with your heart.) Even if you take the job because you really need the money, you'll be doing so with eyes wide open. You will have gained *clarity of intent* with your decision. Often just the *acknowledgment* of your true feelings will relax your stomach.

4. Use your body to help decision-making. For example, in the case above you could use your imagination to see how your body reacts if you *didn't* accept the job. Does the stomach relax? Do you feel lighter? The body never lies. It will give you more of the whole truth on which to make your decisions. This technique of asking the body (the essence of "muscle-testing" that healers use) can be applied to questions both profound as above, or simple, such as what to order at a restaurant.

Though *reason* might try to dismiss those impulses from the body, never doubt your experiences. If you feel sleepy after a meeting, for instance, reason might goad you to carry on like normal. It is not aware that, perhaps, you are processing deep issues at a subconscious level, and you simply need to take a nap to let them unravel on their own. Trust your instincts, and trust your bodily reactions. The body knows. By listening to it, you'll bypass the mind with all its complications, and receive direct signals through the body from your Source in Being.

STILL THE MIND.

The most powerful and direct practice to still the endless chatter of our minds is through meditation, a vast subject with countless variations. All of them, however, have at their core the process of short-circuiting the normal chaos of thoughts that block us from our connection to *Being*. The meditation technique described below stills the mind by placing the attention on cultivating the power of the heart, with which a whole new level of living can begin:

1. Find a comfortable place free of distractions, like a bedroom or garden. Sit comfortably straight with eyes closed. Silently or out loud, call in your Spirit guides as a simple Invocation. Thank them for all they've given you and declare your intent for the meditation session: "I call in all my Spirit Guides to enter this circle. Please accept my gratitude for all the blessings you've given me, and continue to guide, heal and inspire me towards greater levels of love and wisdom…"

2. Place your attention on your breath. As you inhale, visualize it coming into your body and flooding your heart with light and vitality. Exhale, following your breath with attention as it goes out. With the next inhale see your breath again flooding your heart with vitality. In and out, in and out. Keep your attention on your breath going in and out of your heart.

3. If thoughts arise (and they most certainly will!), simply redirect your attention back to breathing into your heart as soon as you notice them. Sometimes, two or three seconds of focused attention can be considered progress. Other times, you'll be able to maintain concentration ten, twenty minutes at a time. When you come out of the meditation, do so gently. Let the stillness and sense of presence permeate your normal daily activities.

4. Do this for a minimum of twenty minutes per session, preferably at the same time every day. When the mind is free of incessant chatter, what remains is presence, or *Being*.

For those of who think, "Nice idea, but I'm way too busy, and don't have time to spare twenty minutes a day," you can remind yourself (your ego) that by bringing your attention on the level of the *cause* of things, you will *perform less and accomplish more*. Ultimately, you'll save time by being much more effective with your actions.

ENTER SACRED SPACE.

Entering "Sacred Space" is a classic process to put aside our ego and formally invite transcendent powers greater than ourselves to guide us in thought, word, and deed. These powers are known as Spirit, Source, Being, Angels, Saints, God(s), or our Illumined Self—any being or force of our own choice that we feel transcends the normal ups and downs of life.

Entering Sacred Space is highly beneficial for any significant event where we want to be at our best physically, mentally, and spiritually. These include launching important projects, opening meetings, beginning daily meditations, conducting marriages, and/or practicing any of these exercises.

Entering Sacred Space can be accomplished through rituals such as lighting candles, drumming, singing, invocations (the calling in of spirits, saints, sages), smudging (the burning of natural herbs such as sage for the smoke that helps spiritual cleansing), or countless other procedures. A crucial element common to all, however, is the *intent* to connect with Spirit:

1. Set up an altar, the physical aspect to a ritual—you are bridging the world of Spirit with that of the physical. You can create an altar by lighting a candle; smudging an area with sage; or arranging mementos, photos of saints, or objects that represent to you something or someone that transcends physical reality.

2. Formally invoke Spirit and/or Spirit guides, ("We call in the saints and sages of all religions…" or "I invoke my Illumined Self…" or "I call in my creative muse for this project….") to enter the space or circle of the ritual.

3. Express gratitude and the *intent* of the ceremony, "Please accept our gratitude for…" and then, "Please guide and inspire us during this ritual, and for this enterprise we are about to begin…"

4. After the event or meeting, release the Spirits, "Thank you, beloved Spirits, and now we release you to your proper abodes knowing you will continue to guide us in our daily life…"

The power of rituals defies reason. Much greater forces are set in motion, so practice *unbending intent*, trust your experiences, and not let your ego or reason dismiss the proceedings. (After all, your ego didn't do such a great job in helping you get what you want; otherwise you would not have been moved to perform the ritual in the first place.)

Also, we don't want to fall into the trap of assuming that just because we performed a ritual, we can become passive and everything will fall in place like magic. Rituals are like planting powerful seeds; we still need to water and feed them with our attention. Alert to impulses from our heart, we will be ever ready to take appropriate action and keep faith that invisible forces are guiding us behind the scenes.

* * *

PRACTICES FOR
DETACHMENT FROM OUTCOMES

This principle is so easy to understand, but so challenging to practice. To master these exercises for detachment requires mental discipline. There is no magic pill, no easy fix except to maintain vigilance against old habits of expecting the world to obey our ego demands. Good luck!

MASTER YOUR OWN ATTENTION.

Directing one's *attention* is an investment of personal power, our valuable *chi*. Where it is invested is where things grow; thus, *a warrior is a master of his or her own attention.* Here are key situations where we can benefit from mindful placement of our attention:

1. If and when you feel anxious, disappointed, or enraged, see if your attention had fallen prey to the world of outcomes—what *might have* happened, or *should have* happened (all concoctions of the ego). If so, detach. Withdraw your attention from *outer* to *inner* events. Refocus from those ego expectations to enjoying the process and keeping faith that "what is truly yours will surely come."

2. Guard against indulging in junk food, junk media, ego demands, or meaningless arguments. Our media and billion–dollar advertisement industry both know full well that to ensnare your attention is to eat your power, money, and resources. Their content is filled with violence, corruption, sex, and scandals to hook your attention. Because they often do nothing but promote fear, cynicism, and despair, be vigilant. Don't squander your *chi;* master your own attention.

3. Bring awareness if and when you have arguments. Some conflicts are valuable because they promote understanding and broad-mindedness. Others go nowhere because you (and your combatant) are both so identified with an opinion that you would rather fight forever than to be proved "wrong." The result, a mindless waste of *chi.* Know the difference. You are not your opinions, so who says you have to win arguments? Withdraw energy from ego demands and refocus it on feeding your soul.

When we become successful in mastering our attention, we find that, ultimately, our well-being depends on nothing outside of ourselves. We will have wakened from the vagaries of the world, wakened from worrying about things beyond our control, and find ourselves free.

ENTHRONE YOUR HEART.

The heart contains the ability to connect us to everything in the universe, to our Source, to loved ones, to strangers, and to our true nature. Our most valuable experiences—inner peace, feelings, beauty, love, joy—reside in our hearts. It should rule on the throne of our being. However, as we have seen, for the vast majority of us (and for society) reason and ego has usurped the royal seat. The consequence? Chronic, needless suffering for individuals, and self-inflicted sabotage of our society. The remedy? Reinstate your heart to the throne:

1. During any moments of upset or anxiety, or situations involving important decisions, ask these questions, "Right now, who is on the throne of my own being?" Reason, or heart? Ego, or my soul? Am I doing something because of love ("I want to go to the party because I'd love to catch up with these people."), or because of fear? ("I want to go to the party because I'm afraid of missing out on important people I should meet.")

2. If you are confused about the answer, trust your intuition, or your inherent wisdom, or a reliable friend to help you gain insight. Once you are willing to explore––"*Something* is bothering me. What? Where am I coming from, head or heart?"—answers begin to come forth. *Ask, and thou shall receive*. You may receive a moment of inspiration, or that trusted friend appears, or you find a book with the essential passage that you needed to hear. Be aware of your *feelings* about the situation more than your thoughts (often filled with judgments, self-pity, and blame).

3. If you discover that you are coming from your heart, go directly to Step 4. If, however, you find that your head is in control, use your power of intent and "reinstate your heart back on the throne." See your situation from the viewpoint of love and compassion, which will often help you see your predicament in a much larger context. Take seriously your feelings, intuition, and dreams, and be open to new insights on your situation.

So, for instance, if you lost your job, the head may spin out of control with worry about lost prestige or bills to pay. (It's only natural.) And yet, viewing the same situation from your heart may reveal that you never liked that job, that you finally have time for your family, and that this moment of lost income has actually stimulated you into starting that labor of love you had dreamed about your entire life.

4. Once Heart is back on the throne and in the position of power, listen to its insights and decisions. *Then* consult with reason as needed to help plan, analyze, and coordinate situations to fulfill your aspirations. *Let reason be a servant to your heart.* For example, in the predicament above with the loss of income, reason may help you realize, for example, that you actually have four months free and clear to reassess your situation and start a new chapter in your life. Enjoy the process.

With the heart back on the throne (along with its allies of feelings, intuition, and dreams), you can now tap the full dimension of your capabilities. Your intuition can once again scour the universe to help find those "jewels" essential for your new journey ahead. *Then* call up your powerful servants, reason and ego, to help you maneuver the tempestuous world of form and time to realize your dream.

ACCEPT WHAT IS.

Whatever happens is perfect, because…it happens. Though we may have no control over the madness of the world, we have infinite control of how we choose to react. So, in spite of the concoctions from our egos (from where most all of our suffering arises), accept all situations. Be like a cork floating down the river— no matter what speed or turmoil there is in the water, it will not get hurt. Even if it becomes submerged, it will not get hurt. With detachment from the world of appearances, and no (inner) resistance to *what is*, we will find a great peace well up from within:

1. If you are struck with adversity, first, *be aware.* It is what it is. Remind your ego that the vast portion of suffering comes *not* from the outer adversity, but from within, e.g., judgments, victimhood, self-importance, false expectations. Be efficient with your *chi,* and focus first on your inner dynamics where the real action occurs. Then take steps accordingly (see below, *Healing the Wounds*).

2. At the outer level of the physical world, choose your course of action. Accepting the situation does not mean that you have to *like* the predicament. If you don't (as with cynical arguments, or certain social groups), *leave.* If it is not possible to

leave (as with certain jobs, or parental responsibilities), *change* the situation first by changing your attitudes and behavior. Then, be vigilant for your quarter centimeter of chance to act, if necessary or possible, to liberate yourself from your predicament. If change is not possible (as in fatal illnesses or loss of a love), *accept* what is.

3. Keep in mind the big picture: Even as you are working on the secondary causes of your life (career, family, projects), ultimate success is measured by how they advance your primary cause—realizing that your true nature transcends all the ups and downs of life.

At the outer level of form, take appropriate action; at the inward level, be detached by accepting *what is*. Be that cork in the river. Simply float on the stream of life through still lakes, tumultuous rapids, or waterfalls with no fears or attachment. Enjoy the miraculous journey of being alive.

DO YOUR BEST, LEAVE THE REST.

In all endeavors, do the best that you are able, given the situation. Remain detached from how the world may or may not approve. It's like watching an infant learning to walk. We don't care if she stumbles or not. We're filled with joy just to see her doing her best. Similarly, our Illumined Self watches us in all our undertakings and sees the passion, heart, and dedication we're able to embody in what we do. Winning and losing, succeeding or failing is of secondary importance:

1. Do your best in any situation. Your "best" takes in account your level of energy, resources, courage, and awareness available at the time. Check that you are not succumbing to laziness, doubt, or lack of courage. Self-discipline counts for a lot here.

2. Be aware that your best is *not* the ego's idealistic fantasy of perfection, an unrealistic goal that opens you to disappointment and self-judgment. Ego often expects you to do *more* than your best, setting another trap that prevents you from living a balanced life.

3. *A warrior picks his battles.* Even though there are many noble conflicts in the world, not all of them are destined for you to fight. To do your best, pick your projects in accordance to impulses from your heart. If you find that your heart is not behind

a particular effort, or your endeavor comes from a sense of obligation (perhaps from parents or peers), choose again. Exercise your free will.

4. Monitor *feelings* about your endeavors. When you know you've done your best, you'll be free from guilt, regrets, and concerns for outside approval. Confidence and peace will flow into you.

Knowing we have truly done our best, we no longer have to be concerned about the results, for the fruits of our labors have been given over to higher authorities. Detached from outcomes, we need only "do our best, and leave the rest," and throw ourselves into the joy of creation.

* * *

PRACTICES FOR
HEALING THE WOUNDS

Most of us are plagued by old issues and pains that have tormented us our entire lives. The following exercises go straight to the heart of the problem—and solution. Those who find the courage to take full responsibility for their own part in their grievances will experience new levels of personal power. Healing our personal wounds is a daunting challenge, but achievable, and the rewards are considerable. Imagine a life with no pain, a life that fills you with creative vitality, gratitude and joy.

EMBRACE YOUR DEMONS.

To truly "know thyself," one must eventually know every aspect of themselves, including those that are the most shameful, ugly, and dark. Acknowledging them in a spirit of love, we can release a tremendous amount of *chi* that, up to this point, has been spent repressing their existence or enduring the pain they've caused. Embracing" them and giving them voice enables true healing to begin.

As we saw earlier, the most debilitating of our inner demons, the ones that cause us the most inner pain are the Judge and the Victim. In the shamanic tradition, a powerful tool for transforming them is called the *Mitoté Book*:

1. Begin the *Mitoté Book*: Obtain a journal that will be dedicated to this practice. On the first page, write down your name, address, date of birth, and any other facts that you would include in a formal document. (The specifics are up to you.). On the second page, write out in your own words a promise to Spirit or your Illumined Self that in this book you will tell the truth, the whole truth, and nothing but the truth, as much as you are able. (No one else reads this book.) Sign and date this vow.

2. On the third page, let the Judge and Victim speak. At the time of your choice, review the day's events. Write in the voice of the Judge all the judgments you made during the day. You don't have to be nice, politically correct, or sensible. You may be vicious, cruel, mean, or unfair. The important thing is to write as you had truly

felt making the judgment. For example,

Judge: "What a know-nothing for a boss... What a goddamn fate, stuck with such a bimbo for a mate… Look at you, with all your higher education and privilege, why aren't you rich by now…?"

The judgments may be against parents, government, God, your boss, and…yourself. Notice that however much you judge the world, it is never as harsh as you judge yourself. By giving voice to your Judge, you release all the emotional and psychological poison that has been stewing within you for perhaps your whole life. Rather than releasing these toxins on to the world randomly (and causing more problems), you now have a dedicated repository for such thoughts. By acknowledging, accepting, and giving voice to even the most ruthless, shameful, ugly aspects of yourself, you will have shifted your perspective from your ego (always ready to pass judgment) to your heart (ever accepting and compassionate). Thus, you begin cultivating unconditional love for yourself, from which all true love begins.

Repeat the procedure for the inner Victim. For example,

Victim: "Ripped off again. Why does this always happen to me? So pathetic, I've screwed up again! I just don't have what it takes…"

3. Do this every day, letting the Judge and Victim have their say. After a few weeks, months, years, you'll notice the same old patterns, the same old complaints repeating themselves endlessly. (It's so deplorable it can make you laugh, but at least it's all out in the open.) After a few more months, you'll notice that their volume may lessen. Or that the criticisms have turned mostly against yourself. Observe these changes with no judgment.

4. After at least a few months of Step 2 and 3, talk to your Judge and Victim by writing a dialogue in your *Mitoté Book*. Ask each why it continually judges you. What would make it happy? What would it like you to do to make it stop judging everything? Explain to the Judge the distinction between *discernment* between truth and illusion (which you would always value and appreciate), and *judgment* between good and evil (for which you have no more patience), because it only makes you feel guilty and small. Anyway, who are we to judge?

5. Make a new agreement with your Judge explaining that you will always value its power of discernment, but that you will have no more tolerance for its indictments. Explain to the Victim the distinction between *forbearance,* the ability to endure adversity and suffer nobly the rough and tumble of life, and *victimhood,* the indulgence of weakness and self-pity. Similarly as you did with the Judge, renegotiate a new agreement of its role for you.

When you *practice* this procedure, you'll find, as many do, that the *Mitoté Book* becomes something you look forward to engaging in every day. Where else is there a place to have your say exactly as you feel, ugly as it may be? It becomes your best listener, your personal therapist (and you don't have to pay a thing). Repeat this procedure for a few months, and when you feel ready, renegotiate your agreement with these two demons. You will be transforming them to a higher purpose, and thus turning the deepest darkest aspects of yourself into light. With no Judge and Victim, your life will shift fundamentally, and you will fill with a joy beyond understanding.

FORGIVE.

Forgiveness is the most powerful act for cleansing our emotional body. All the anger and despair we may hold from betrayal, injustice, abuse, and neglect builds and builds until we are filled with emotional poison that only prolongs our suffering. The best antidote to this toxicity is forgiveness, an act that will leave you feeling clean and light. Here is a Forgiveness Ritual involving Ritual Burning:

1. Write a statement of who and what you would like to forgive. Describe the situation and express your misgiving, and the statement of pardon. For example, "I forgive my ex for lying about me, and turning my kids against me. She was reacting in anger, and didn't really know what she was doing…"

   Don't forget to also forgive yourself: "And I forgive myself for ignoring our family, and causing my ex to feel years of neglect. I promise I'll never be so blind again with anyone. I, too, didn't know what I was doing."

2. Address the expected complaints from your ego that such mercy is weakness, and that you're letting someone off the hook. (This can be done either as an internal dialogue during meditation, or through writing.) Remind your ego that forgiveness is not about letting someone get away with something, but rather it's about restoring your original sense of well-being.

3. Release your written statement to Spirit through Ritual Burning. Prepare an open fire—fire bowl, fireplace, or a candle in a metal pot. Enter Sacred Space. Then, place your written statement into the fire. Watch every bit of the paper burn and go up in smoke. See the image as a fitting symbol of the complete dissolution of your old grievances.

4. Remain vigilant against the ego's tendency to fall into old patterns by reopening old wounds. Quite often, the perpetrators who maligned you suffered abusive conditioning just like you; given their level of awareness at the time, they like you did the best they knew how. With compassion and understanding, enjoy the process. This practice is a profound practice for cleansing your emotional body.

Repeat this process as necessary. Old grievances die hard. Forgiveness is *not* about the thinking mind weighing out wrongdoings or dispensing punishments. It's about regaining feelings of compassion, peace, and joy.

REWRITE PERSONAL HISTORY.

History is but a description of a dream, open to continual change and reinterpretation. Our personal history, too, intertwined with that of our family's, is also but a subjective interpretation of what happened during early formative years.

Much of our suffering comes from assuming as true what is actually our subjective memory of events. For example, a friend was known as the "black sheep of the family." Unfortunately, he (unconsciously) accepted this family myth as true; after forty years he still feels bitter about not getting a fair shake from an unjust world. This history was "true" as long he believed in it. However, our history can just as easily be erased when we recognize that this history is malleable, that it's kept in place only because we believe in it.

To free ourselves from old belief structures, wounds and habits that hinder our well-being, we have the technique of Rewriting Personal History:

1. Write down the "story" that caused the pain, and describing the emotional wound. For example, "I was consistently judged and beaten by my mother, and my father was never around, so I always felt alienated and turned to art as the only activity that felt safe."

2. After writing down the existing story, use the power of your imagination and see the whole scenario from the viewpoint of Spirit, your Illumined Self. Trust your intuitive wisdom, and rewrite that history. (If you get stuck, write with your opposite hand.) From this transcendent viewpoint, remind yourself that in every tragedy there is a treasure and your job is to find it. So, for instance, "My neglect by parents, though painful, allowed me to develop an independent mind that has proven so important for my work as an artist. Those beatings instilled in me a fortitude to keep going amidst all adversity, which I indeed am capable of..."

3. Again, using your imagination, *feel* what it would be like to actually have lived this new history. Does it make you feel like a tragic romantic? Bitter? Angry? Heroic? Rewrite the history until you feel joyous, wise, creative, loving, and grateful. Trust your feelings. There is no right or wrong; it's *not* about reason, not about the facts, per se, but about the *interpretation* of these facts.

4. When you feel good about your new history, memorize it. Make it so that whenever the old patterns arise, you will automatically replace them with this new dream.

As you rewrite your story, the "facts" may or may not be the same. It may be "a lie that reveals the truth," (as Picasso said about his own paintings). What *is* important is how this new interpretation makes you feel, how it transforms you from a position of a victim to one of power. Knowingly or not, people redesign themselves, adopt new names and reinterpret facts about their life all the time for all kinds of purposes. The objective of "Rewriting Personal History," though, is to have us wake up from the "dream of the planet" beginning with our families. We can then become co-creators with Spirit of our own destiny. As we quoted before from Shakespeare, "Nothing is either good or bad, but thinking makes it so."

FEEL THE FEELINGS, DROP THE STORIES.

The unpredictability of life, especially nowadays, has led to sudden setbacks and tragedies for many people. Though we know we should be detached, and accept *what is*, we may still find ourselves filled with disappointment, rage, or grief. Adversity has breached our first level of defense—detachment, knowing how it's all illusion—and worked its way inside us. We feel terrible. What's the best course of action? The solution is a secondary line of defense, a most efficient technique to process our misgivings: *Feel the feelings, drop the stories:*

1. Assume a meditation position. Shut your eyes, and enter Sacred Space (see above). Place full attention on your feelings and how they impact the body. (*I feel so depressed, heaviness in my chest, growling in the stomach, tears in the eyes*). What are the textures, the colors, the densities you feel? (*That dark gray mass inside my chest feels like heavy goo. And my stomach feels prickly with fire. I'm so angry!*). If there is one area that seems especially intense, imagine yourself sitting right in the middle of it: (*I'm in the middle of fire, consumed by rage…It's warming my whole body, my shoulders…*). Allow sufficient time to fully experience your feelings.

2. Should thoughts come up with complaints, indignation, or judgments—*"Why do they always blame me…?" "How dare she try to…?" "I trusted him, but he took advantage of my kindness, and…."*—withdraw your attention from these "stories" and refocus it on feelings and how they affect your body. Be *present* with the ache. As with physical wounds, once these psychic wounds have been "dressed" there is nothing to do but to let nature take its course for its healing.

3. Be patient, observe how the feelings change. Nothing is permanent; everything of the manifest world passes in its own good time. With no thoughts keeping them in place, feelings will begin to transform on their own, (*"Now, the dark goo is turning a lighter blue. I feel water in my eyes, I feel so sad..."*). Typically, depression can turn into anger, anger turn into sadness, sadness into compassion, and compassion into …boredom. (*Now, I feel bored. Why am I sitting here when I can dive back into my project?*) Or peace. In any case, your original angst will have been transformed. When you have regained your balance and feel revitalized, rejoin daily life.

4. Honor yourself for your vigilance, for your success in divine alchemy. Take yourself out to lunch for how well you handled adversity.

By feeling our feelings, we no longer remain in denial of our experiences, favorable or not. By dropping the stories, we become free of the mental structures that keep debilitating feelings in place. If *detachment* served as the first line of defense against adversity affecting our well-being, then this practice can be seen as the second line of defense. Any "negative" feelings that get through to plague us from within can be handled most efficiently when we *feel the feelings, and drop the stories.*

* * *

ABOUT THE AUTHOR

Fu-Ding Cheng—visionary filmmaker and shamanic artist—began his career as a practicing architect, but has since focused his attention on books, films, and spirituality. In 1990, he founded *Liquid Light Productions* devoted to explore paths of self-illumination and mystical adventures through books, films, art and seminars.

His multi-faceted artistic career includes a prize-winning series of films, *Zen-Tales for the Urban Explorer* presented as a special retrospective at the Hammer Museum, album covers (Heart's *Dog and Butterfly*); and a children's book, *Dream-House*. While teaching film directing at the North Carolina School of the Arts, he created a groundbreaking new curriculum, "*Shamanic Tools for the Filmmaker*."

However, first priority over all vocational activities has been his life-long devotion to the spiritual quest, which led him to journeys East (meditation in the Himalayas, Chinese Kung-Fu), and to journeys West (spiritual-psychology, Meso-American shamanic practice). In 1995, through breakthrough experiences working with teacher/shaman don Miguel Ruiz (*The Four Agreements*), he "Jumped to the Sun," and nothing has been quite the same since. He has woken up to...*what is*. His life is now filled with joy and peace unassailable by outside events.

Through books, art, public speaking, and seminars, Fu-Ding has been inspired to share practical pathways to personal freedom for everyone. *Map of Desire*, a blueprint for self-fulfillment, is his latest work towards spreading the deepest wisdom for the widest number of people. For more information, please visit, www.fudingcheng.com and facebook.com/MapofDesire.

* * *

CPSIA information can be obtained at www.ICGtesting.com
Printed in the USA
BVOW10s0104310315

393730BV00001BA/1/P